Praise for

The Value Factor

How Global Leaders Use Information
for Growth and Competitive Advantage

Mark Hurd and Lars Nyberg

"**A must read for busy executives looking for every advantage for their firm.** In this book, tech giant NCR's Hurd and Nyberg show how to turn often overlooked and undervalued information into a super-performing asset."

MICHAEL TREACY
Author of *Double-Digit Growth* and *The Discipline of Market Leaders*

"It's called 'The Information Age' for a reason. Information, even more than capital assets, products, or brands, will be the best source of sustainable competitive advantage. In this book, Nyberg and Hurd have succeeded in outlining a vision and a plan for putting that information to work in ways that drop directly to the bottom line. **Better read it if you plan to do any business in the 21st century.**"

DON PEPPERS AND MARTHA ROGERS
Founders, Peppers & Rogers Group
Authors of *The One to One Future*

"In *The Value Factor,* Mark Hurd and Lars Nyberg bring us a fresh perspective on some of **the most important, common sense factors that have enabled companies to better leverage data for competitive advantage and business success.**"

RANDY MOTT
Senior Vice President and CIO, Dell

"Congratulations to authors Hurd and Nyberg who show us how leaders maximize excellence by maximizing the value of information with every decision. **It's the only way to see the road ahead while doing business at the speed of light.**"

DIPAK C. JAIN
Dean, Kellogg School of Management, Northwestern University

"***The Value Factor* is every executive's competitive edge.** It provides unique perspectives from top global businesses. Implementing these strategic tools and insights will position your company to obtain boundless growth and profitability."

BILL MILNES
President and CEO, Blue Cross & Blue Shield of Vermont

THE VALUE FACTOR

THE VALUE FACTOR

How Global Leaders Use
Information for Growth and
Competitive Advantage

Mark Hurd and **Lars Nyberg**

Bloomberg PRESS

PRINCETON

This publication contains the authors' opinions and is designed to provide accurate and authoritative information. It is sold with the understanding that the authors, publisher, and Bloomberg L.P. are not engaged in rendering legal, accounting, investment-planning, or other professional advice. The reader should seek the services of a qualified professional for such advice; the authors, publisher, and Bloomberg L.P. cannot be held responsible for any loss incurred as a result of specific investments or planning decisions made by the reader.

All the corporate case studies in this book are based on personal interviews with senior executives at the companies and/or public record information.

Printed in the United States of America

First edition published 2004

1 3 5 7 9 10 8 6 4 2

Library of Congress Cataloging-in-Publication Data

Hurd, Mark
  The value factor : how global leaders use information for growth and competitive advantage / Mark Hurd and Lars Nyberg.
    p. cm.
Includes index.
  ISBN 1-57660-157-9 (alk. paper)
1. Business information services. 2. Information resources management. 3. Business intelligence.
I. Nyberg, Lars. II. Title.

HF54.5.H87 2004
658.4'038—dc22   2003024265

Table of Contents

Foreword

Ask children what they know about the Brachiosaurus and chances are you'll learn it is the dinosaur that had two brains. The idea of an animal so huge that it handed off control of its back legs and tail to a second brain is just about irresistible to young people. They are caught up, no doubt, by the opportunities it presents for denial of responsibility. While paleontologists these days prefer to play down the second brain as no more than a lump on the dinosaur's spinal cord, it's too late to take back the image. A giant body with two minds that wrestle for control is too handy a metaphor.

It is a metaphor often applied to firms, and not without cause. A large enterprise learns a lot in the course of a day, and must act on much of it right away. Sometimes it acts before there is time to form a single coherent picture of events, and the image of a dinosaur with its head at cross-purposes to its hindquarters springs irresistibly to mind.

This book is about organizations that have decided to be single-minded. Its stories show what can be achieved when corporations put the very highest priority on pulling together all available information to form one, and only one, picture of what's going on. No matter how vast their scale, how much information they must digest, or how dispersed their decision-making, these modern global firms take care not to fall victim to multiple contradictory interpretations of reality. They see the best possible view of their markets, their supply lines and themselves, and they give that view to every decision maker who needs it. The result, as you will see in the stories that follow, is not merely efficiency, though that's not to be scoffed at. The result of superior vision is often a radically superior business model. In the land of the blind, everyone flies the airline with the one-eyed pilots.

Better information, then, transforms the business. The transformation stories in this book that I like the most, given my own particular research interests, are the customer ecosystem stories. They show what happens to markets when customers discover that they are no longer undifferentiated ciphers in crowded marketplaces and workplaces, but are remembered and can command a vendor's attention for who they are, what they alone want and what they are worth to the vendor. Customers want identity. They don't want to be members of segments—they want to be acknowledged for their quirks, for themselves. The vendors with the best information systems give customers just that—the richest, most validating identities.

Better information also transforms the terms of collaboration between businesses. From these stories we learn that the more we can see, the less we have to own to be in control. We see how a single accurate and complete view of the supply chain has liberated enterprises from the burdens of massive vertical integration. "The supply chain has dissolved into a series of inter-company relationships," write the authors, pointing to the inevitable result of a single common view of what's going on.

Read these accounts of life on the frontier of the information economy, for inspiration, for edification and for an exhilarating sense of how the liberating power of information can do for our world what mechanical power did for the world of previous generations. Mark Hurd and Lars Nyberg show us the future, and it is amazing!

John A. Deighton
Harold M. Brierley Professor
of Business Administration
Harvard Business School

Acknowledgments

This book would not have been possible without the great work and cooperation of the whole Teradata team. So many of our Teradata clients gave generously of their time to speak to us about the successes and challenges of their companies' information resource strategies. Under the leadership of Mike Koehler, the Teradata sales team provided expert counsel and through their close working relationships with clients facilitated those essential links. The industry analysts, our partners and marketing team as well as a host of Teradata friends and associates around the world were a constant source of ideas and creative energy. We are fortunate to work with such a special team. At the time of writing, Mark Hurd was President and COO of Teradata, a division of NCR. Since that time he has taken on the leadership of NCR and passed the mantle of Teradata leadership on to Mike Koehler. We know that under Mike's guidance, Teradata's clients will continue to flourish, providing new case studies for future editions of this book.

VALUE

1

Capitalize on Your Information

Have you realized the full value of the most important resource in your company?

TowerGroup

We operate in a fast-changing global business environment. As Mark Sievewright, President and CEO of TowerGroup says, we're all short on time now and the time deprivation means companies need to adapt to new and different ways of interacting. Staying ahead of the competition is only getting harder. The tipping point between success and failure is a razor's edge, the thinnest margin between winning and losing. Build a better widget. Our competitors can copy and improve on the widget before we even begin to capitalize on our edge.

We need to extract more value from what we have. How do we do this? Cutting costs is a double-edged sword. We need to be lean to succeed. But we need to invest to innovate, to evolve, to compete and to lead.

Experts Say

Klaus Schwab, President of the Davos World Economic Forum, observed recently, "We have moved from a world where the big eat the small to a world where the fast eat the slow."

So, we need to change the rules. What is the only thing I have that my competitors do not have? What can I invest in that my competitors cannot replicate? The answer—information.

> Capitalize on the information
> you own about your customers,
> suppliers and partners;
> it is the new value proposition
> for sustainable long-term growth.

Build a quieter washing machine, a smoother running car, a more comfortable plane or a faster package delivery service. A quality product is the table stakes. Our competitors can copy us. Virtually every industry is commoditizing. As much as we'd like to believe that our product is superior and unique, the reality is that the differences between one product and a competitor's is a nuance a customer may not even discern. But if we use the information we have that our competitors don't have to enhance the value proposition for our customers, then we have something competitive for the long term.

Turn the tables for a minute. As a customer, is it worth something to us that a company knows us? Of course it is. If an airline remembers we like window seats and are vegetarian, it is of value. If our bank's ATM knows how much we habitually withdraw from which account, bypasses the standard string of questions and instead asks immediately if we would like the "usual," it is of value. We don't go to the corner diner for the best food. We go because they know us and we don't even have to look at the menu. And "customer" does not just mean the end consumer; it is every partner or supplier a company deals with up and down the supply chain. If a company knows how many tubes of its toothpaste are selling at the stores it supplies and it can avoid stock-outs, that information is of value. If a company understands the maintenance cycle on its planes and their parts suppliers can coordinate more tightly with its needs, it is of value. The value of knowing our customers rolls up from the corner diner to the largest corporations.

We can already own and easily store the information we need. All the data is there for our collection. If we're not collecting and analyzing all the information we can, the competitive gap will only widen. In many industries data volume is doubling every eight to twelve months. The accretion of data increases exponentially every year. We are in an information age. Not only because of the Internet and the proliferation of media sources, but because every company is an information company now. The single fastest growing resource in every business is data. The wealth of information at our disposal grows every day. We can, in fact we have to, take advantage of its extraordinary value.

Five major forces drive this phenomenon:

- Increased granularity in customer and transaction detail
- Cumulative volume of historical data
- Access to a broader range of demographic data
- Addition of new clickstream data
- Mergers and acquisitions

Growth and Value

The sheer volume of data at our disposal can either bury us or propel us. It's our choice. To ignore our data resources is fatal. Truly sustainable growth is only possible if we are able to leverage resources more efficiently in order to make better decisions faster and less expensively. Productivity, return on investment, operating efficiency, or whatever name we choose to call it, needs to increase by orders of magnitude. To maintain a competitive edge requires constant, geometric productivity increases. Increases only achievable by unlocking the value of our information capital. Information—clean, correct, complete, up-to-date data—needs to be immediately and readily accessible to those who need it most, when they need it. Only then is the competitive productivity gain assured.

Bank of America As early as 1989 Bank of America envisioned the day it would operate based on a single version of the truth. Instead of wasting time sorting through multiple sources of data, Bank of America envisioned using information as a new engine of growth. As the company moved from an acquisition orientation to a growth orientation, the focus shifted to finally realizing that vision of a single source for data. The task of cleaning and consolidating the disparate information sources in the company has just begun, but conservative estimates are that a 20 percent increase in productivity has been achieved already. That number is only going to look better as Bank of America continues to unlock the value of its information resources.

The growth trend is already there—human productivity has increased dramatically over the past decade. Economists at the Federal Reserve have identified a direct relationship between increased labor productivity and rising share prices since the early 1990s. The bottom line is that we all want higher share prices. We want our success to be reflected in the market.

> *One Wall Street expert has argued* **Experts Say** *that a company's share price is a brand unto itself, reflecting the value-creating ability of the CEO and the enterprise. Brand building is tough. We want to protect what we've built.*

Why is productivity increased when we begin to mine the value of our information capital? We gain control of decisions and outcomes. The result is increased efficiency and the kind of reliability the market recognizes. Boards and investors don't like surprises. Surprises disrupt the momentum of a company and can destroy value. The market rewards companies who deliver what they say they will. But change is a fact of life in today's complex business environment.

To rise to the challenge and the opportunity of change, we need to have a complete view of our company, a single view of the business. How? Have all our information in one place, in one understandable form, accessible to those who need it, when they need it to make the right decisions now. The technology already exists to make this possible. It is no more than the tool. The more important question is whether we have the vision to commit to using our information to drive growth. If we want to stay competitive, it isn't a choice.

> *There's been a paradigm shift in* **Experts Say** *the way companies view their information resources. We've moved from a view of dependence and utility to one of criticality.*

> **Ed Glotzbach**
> CIO
> SBC

Experts Say

At FedEx the information about the package is as important as the package itself.

Fred Smith
Founder
FedEx Corp.

Customers are the only reason a firm exists. And the best way to grow the company is to increase the value of each customer to the company.

**Don Peppers and
Martha Rogers**
Founders
Peppers and Rogers Group

We were thinking about data before "data warehouse" became part of the vernacular. We resolved to look at information as a competitive weapon.

Martin Lippert
CIO and Vice Chair
RBC

Why base our decision-making on assumptions? We can know, not guess. And we can act now on the knowledge and information we have. Travelocity is already doing it.

Travelocity

When Travelocity heard that TWA had established a special low fare from L.A. to San Juan, Puerto Rico, it quickly identified all of its L.A. region customers who had inquired about Puerto Rico fares and e-mailed them the information the next morning. 25 percent of those e-mailed purchased the TWA ticket, or another ticket to the Caribbean, an astonishingly high direct-marketing response. Travelocity's information is earning high returns.

Every company needs to get holistic.

The speed and complexity of competitive decision-making requires us to have deep and immediate access to our information capital. Increasingly businesses are asking "impossible" questions: questions that draw on information from across a company—market basket analysis combined with weather patterns; the most profitable locations for planes on any day given advance bookings, anticipated same-day passengers and the overbooking allowance; the profitability implications of delivering Package A late vs. Package B. Think of how many times we've asked those kinds of questions and been told there was no answer, or if there was an answer we could have it soon…next month, not now, when we need it.

The productivity breakthroughs are not going to come from running faster computers. The right technology is an essential tool, but it is never sufficient. The true breakthroughs come from more creative brains using our company's information capital.

> Realizing the value in the
> brainpower of the knowledge
> worker is the real source
> of productivity breakthroughs
> and company growth.

Our information allows us to get closer to the customers, suppliers, partners, employees, various divisions in our company and ultimately the market. Information is our corporate "sight." In a fast-changing world like ours it is critical to eliminate blind spots. The economy is changing. So is the way we do business, our competitors' businesses and the geopolitical landscape. The market rewards agility. The best CEOs are managing the future.

Harnessing the horsepower of a company's information, or business intelligence, should be a closed loop system. The goal is to create a system that replicates the process by which individuals make decisions every day.

TDWI   Wayne Eckerson, Director of
Education and Research at The
Data Warehousing Industry, TDWI, describes it this way. A
business intelligence strategy consists of a five-step cycle: gather,
analyze, plan, act and review. This is the same process that human
beings employ to make decisions.

The job of business analysis, Eckerson says, used to be the
specialized responsibility of an elite group of analysts.
Increasingly it is becoming a job for everyone. That means the
information needs to be at everyone's fingertips. Feeding and
managing the continuous cycle of gathering, analyzing, planning,
acting and reviewing enables a company constantly to fine-tune
the business intelligence process.

Every decision a person makes is based on the accumulation of all
the experiences they have ever had. As experiences accumulate,
a person subconsciously, or consciously, builds inner rules for
dealing with a variety of situations. Each subsequent experience,
decision and outcome feeds back into the process, enabling a
person to reassess, refine or rebuild their inner decision-making
rules, Eckerson says.

A human being's ability to act spontaneously, flexibly and yet
wisely in new situations is simply the result of well-honed rules
that have been refined through a lifetime of experiences. The
ideal business intelligence system should operate the same way,
Eckerson says.

Optimizing decision-making requires companies to make information
available to those who need it now. Protracted historical analysis is only
a start and is largely ineffective in this economic environment where
speed and precision are valued.

Invest in Your Information Capital

Information is the most important untapped resource in your company. Invest in it. You probably already have the innovative, analytical thinkers, the knowledge workers who can mine the information for new profit opportunities and be the engine of higher productivity.

Many companies suffer because information is hoarded in scattered silos, fragmented by division, department, region and a host of other organizational categories. Siloed information breeds inconsistency, which in turn leads to fatal inaccuracy and hinders the execution of any strategy. Some companies hemorrhage profits every year as a result. Needless to say, this approach to information is bad for productivity. Not only that, inconsistency leads to a slow, but steady, erosion of a company's credibility among its customers, suppliers and eventually the market.

Fragmented information sources means inferior information, an insurmountable obstacle even for the best minds. When the same information is available to everyone who needs it, it represents a trusted single version of the truth. The information is usable and valuable.

Consider these three key areas of business and the strategic opportunities of effectively used information: the customer relationship, the logistics of supply chain and price management, and financial and management reporting.

Customers

Leveraging our information capital enables us to achieve a holistic view of our customers. A bank customer with a mortgage, credit card, checking account and money market account should be treated as one customer, not four. It's a win-win outcome. The customer, consciously or not, assigns a value to being known and understood. And the company realizes higher returns because it is better able to serve its customers. Understanding the total profitability picture of each customer enables us to set effective strategies to increase that profitability.

Fubon Group

Fubon Group, a major Chinese financial holding company consisting of banking, insurance, securities, direct marketing and other subsidiaries, has a five-year plan for getting closer to its customers. Fubon Group knows that seeing each of its customers as "one" across the company has value on the bottom line. A holistic view will enable better risk management with full portfolio analysis of customers, better wealth management, better contact management and more effective marketing.

Supply Chain Logistics

Information is essential to achieving a multidimensional view of our business. Knowing in real-time the detail of shipments in progress, production levels, pricing, sales and inventory will put us closer to the market. We can take control of the business process, anticipate problems before they occur and manage the future. Superior logistics adds up.

Controlling operations often means making difficult decisions quickly and adjusting strategy in real-time to avoid bleeding revenue. Continental Airlines is a model of agility.

Continental Airlines

On September 15, 2001, Continental Airlines knew that it would need to cut at least 20 percent of its workforce in order to deal with the crisis in the airline industry precipitated by the events of September 11.

Because of its mastery of its information resources, Continental was able to absorb the impact of the tragedy immediately into its business planning. The airline differentiated bookings made prior to September 11 and those made after, and applied metrics to each that calculated the possibility of a no-show. Continental management was able to integrate this data with information about where its planes were scheduled to be and where they might be more valuable. They were able to combine booking information with logistics information to gain a more complete picture of the airline's situation during the crisis.

The first week was triage to save the airline from going out of business. Then came the quick and critical decision about resource allocation. 20 percent of the schedule needed to be cut. At least 20 percent of costs had to go, too. Continental leveraged its information capital to make decisions about where to reroute planes, cancel flights and reassign employees.

The airline suffered economically, of course. But Continental's losses were a fraction of the losses suffered by its competitors. Over the long term, Continental will call on its information resources to analyze the way its business might need to change to reflect the economic climate. Continental will use its information to question everything about how people fly; even the hub and spokes model is up for review. The only thing that won't change is the basic vision of the company—what product do people value, will they pay for and how can it be delivered profitably?

Financial Reporting

Financial and management strategy is a continuous process of information gathering, analysis and decision-making. Established goals, plans and strategies need to adapt to changes. Knowing what was, what is and what if means we are flexible enough to respond to the unexpected. To be dependable requires being adaptable. No question, the public trust has been eroded. CEOs are increasingly accountable for the timeliness and accuracy of their results. Better insight into our business also means better oversight. What the market trusts, the market rewards.

Each of these profit opportunities is leveraged by having a single version of the truth—one complete view of the customer, of the supply chain, of finance and management. Current information must be linked to historical information and both must be equally accessible. History does repeat itself—the future is the past returning through another gate. Managing the future, avoiding surprises and creating value require access to rich information from across the company and through time.

Customers are more than a series of unrelated transactions. Each is an accumulation of all the transactions they have ever had. Logistics can only be mastered when past performance and future capacity are looked at together. Financial performance is empty of meaning if it contains only one snapshot of a particular moment in time and a backward-looking metric at that.

How to unlock the value of our information capital is the most important strategic challenge facing us today. Each of these information sources is a piece of the puzzle. Integrating the information across the company is the first important step.

CEO Leadership

The corporate scene is much changed from what is was even a decade ago. Dispersed management structures are the flavor of the month. Business schools teach tomorrow's managers to drive decision-making down through the organization. Yet flattened corporate structures, for all their agility and responsiveness, can actually pose a serious challenge to the implementation of a single strategic vision. Information flow naturally follows decision-making. Who "owns" the information often decides the direction of the corporation or business unit.

Before long, local managers in distant markets are making crucial decisions based on information to which they alone have access. At corporate headquarters we may be totally unaware of what information is being acted on. Business unit managers become possessive of clients, contacts and information. Information and communication technologies are used to create cumbersome and expensive data silos, instead of being the basis of smart systems—broad-based, integrated, single-truth decision systems.

Information capital is being used against our strategy, not in support of it. Individuals hoard data, supposedly in pursuit of their "right" to autonomous decision-making and unhampered creativity. And while it is true that individual creativity is the source of much richness in the arts and sciences of our society, companies are not primarily creative endeavors. To realize its vision, a company must synchronize the efforts of all its moving parts. Only then can it execute its strategy with consistent success. Creating a system that works is the most important act of the CEO.

An unpleasant surprise faced by some of us is that our company's technology—originally intended to enhance the system and increase efficiency and productivity—can actually become an obstacle to overall business success. When we ask a question there are no answers, or worse, there are five different answers because information systems are not linked. Widespread decision-making authority without a clear, consistent, unified view of the entire business enterprise poses serious risks for bottom-line results.

Leveraging our information capital means unhitching management structure from information ownership. How? Have a strong controlling vision. Reward collaboration. Enable decision-making.

As the senior leadership we know that vision is one thing that cannot be delegated, but implementation of the vision, ensuring that it penetrates to every level of the company, can and should be. Leaders set the goals, but everyone else must be in synch if the company has any hope of meeting them. Like any good team, everyone needs to be working toward the same goal. Strong leadership is the first ingredient for a strong team, and together they are a powerful combination.

Turbulent Market Strategy

Managing through a period of economic fluctuation presents a special set of problems for senior business executives. In the past, companies reacted to market downturns with layoffs, hoarding cash and delaying innovation and the introduction of new products. Three sure bets for a slow recovery.

Management faces three challenges during and immediately after a recession:

1. Streamline the business without unnecessary cutting. Trim non-critical costs and evaluate marginal businesses and relationships with a view to eliminating the weakest. Broad cost cutting, as an end in itself, is at best a short-term response that can result in a hollowed out company. Instead, smart leaders assess the return on each dollar spent and eliminate investments in assets with the least potential. Maintaining a healthy return on investment requires constant innovation, not wholesale cost cutting.

2. Protect and invest in the most valuable employees, the most productive customer relationships and industry innovations.

3. Continue to provide leadership and vision and make sure that every employee throughout the business has the tools to implement that vision.

All three of these challenges are best met by investing in the information capital of the company. We can't get off the market roller coaster, but we can smooth the ride by planning and investing in the future, even when times are tough.

Market Demands

In bull or bear markets, the economy is a demanding and unforgiving environment. Accelerated market dynamics impose new pressures on companies. Compressed business cycles and increasingly complex business decisions put a premium on the need to use information effectively.

Business cycles used to last 20 or 30 years. But as the economy has grown in size, scope and sheer complexity, business cycles have compressed dramatically. Recessions are shorter. Recoveries need to be quicker. In order to respond to the constant performance pressures, companies need to make decisions faster and easier or risk falling behind their competitors. Federal Reserve Chairman Alan Greenspan has said that the "substantial improvement of access of business decision makers to real-time information" has played a key role in keeping the economy in a milder recession and allowing a quicker comeback. Leveraging your information capital is the key to success.

How Do We Do It?

We started this chapter with a question—have you realized the full value of the most important resource in your company? The answer, for most of us, is probably not. We know information is a valuable resource, but we haven't extracted the value. So how do we do it?

- Capitalization on information resources
- Leadership vision
- Leadership commitment to implementation
- Collaborative corporate culture
- Internal and external relationship ecosystems

Realizing the full value of our information resources is a long-term project that demands commitment and innovative thinking. In the next chapters we'll look at how a broad range of companies have begun to tackle the issue.

VISION

2

Leadership
for
Success

Vision is the strategic underpinning of any success. More than simply a road map to company strategy, vision is the philosophy of corporate leadership. The strength and clarity of our vision will dictate its success. The best corporate vision becomes part of a company's DNA, but first it is part of the leaders' DNA. As Ghandi said, "Be the change you want in the world."

> Envision the future of
> your industry and get there first.

Act Global

Vision is global. Myopia equals mediocrity. As successful executives we have to create and foster a global mentality—a global vision and a global strategy.

Global used to mean multinational. Not anymore. The definition has expanded. It is not about how many countries a company operates in. A global company is one that collaborates effectively across the entire organization, whether worldwide or in one country.

> A company is truly global when
> every person who deals with it,
> internally and externally,
> sees one *single* version of the truth.

The global success of any vision depends upon the consistency with which the vision is applied across operations. The more we, as leaders of our companies, pay attention to core operations the more opportunity we have to support our vision.

Business success is as much about profits as it is about ethos and philosophy. The core of a company's operations is the culture embodied in the leadership vision. Cultural change needs to happen to empower employees, partners, suppliers and customers. Only then will a company have one vision and *one team* to make it a reality.

As leaders, our priorities and values set the tone for the rest of the organization. Creating more value from existing resources, constantly improving productivity, steadily increasing return on investment, and ensuring a controlled, no-surprises environment. From strongly supported institutional values, everything else follows naturally.

We talk about vision a lot, but what *is* it?

A vision is the stated strategic intent of a company, the strategic blueprint for managing now and into the future and changing industry rules. Vision is the foundation on which leaders build *control* over operations and ultimately create *value* across the enterprise. Top organizations are the best in their class because they have one idea, one vision *originating from the leaders* that is central to every decision made throughout the organization.

Charles Schwab

Charles Schwab understands the need for leadership vision. Some years ago, Schwab, who then ran a small upstart brokerage established in the 1970s, committed himself and his company to providing the highest levels of customer service possible, more channels to choose from and more flexibility. Charles Schwab's personal commitment to that vision provided the drive his company needed to put it at the top of its industry. On the way he created new industry standards that forced the old established firms to rethink their business models.

A slogan is not a vision. Saying "we want to make money and sell product" is not a vision. Saying "we want to be the best" is not a vision—best at what? A successful vision is aspirational, inspirational and specific enough to be easily understood by all the stakeholders in a company—employees, customers, investors, partners and the market.

AMR Research, Inc. Bob Parker, Vice President of Enterprise Commerce Management Strategies at AMR Research, Inc., highlights four highly successful companies, whose single specific focus (their *vision*) enabled them to achieve leadership positions in their markets.

- Dell Computer's motto "be direct" sums up Dell's whole ethos—direct to customers, direct with each other internally and direct with suppliers externally.
- Wal-Mart's "everyday low prices" informs every move the company makes.
- Charles Schwab "empowers individual investors" like no investment company did before it.
- FedEx is "worldwide on time" and has set the standard to which its competitors must rise.

Where does vision come from? It comes from understanding the intricacies of the particular industry in which a company operates. It comes down to information. The more a company's leaders know about the business they're in, the better able they are to set goals that can take their organization into the future. Leaders who understand their company's financial operations, customer's needs, supplier and partner relationships and what motivates employees will be the leaders to envision the future of their industries.

Implement the Vision

A vision is only as good as its implementation. In large corporations there are generally two major roadblocks—fragmentation and inertia. They are really part and parcel of the same critical problem—multiple views of the business.

Our company, NCR, operates in
over 100 countries and was, until a

few years ago, structured on a country-by-country basis. The company had operations around the world but they weren't efficiently collaborating.

As each country made decisions about how to run "their" business, strategies became localized and the infrastructure and processes became fragmented. Many different operational systems developed causing the finance department, for example, to spend an inordinate amount of time sifting and standardizing information. It was nearly impossible, within a reasonable time frame, for NCR to get a complete view of receivables, travel and entertainment expenses, inventory and other aspects of the company's financial picture.

The inertial force of being such a large organization made it difficult—but we had to make some hard changes. The country division model was broken down and NCR centralized its financial functions into a shared service center model. This model consolidated the operational finance functions for the entire company into four locations through which all activity is now managed. Most of the disparate operational systems have been collapsed into global systems. The resulting standardized data is being loaded multiple times a day into one integrated Enterprise Data Warehouse for reporting and analysis.

Now managers in the company can get a faster, clearer view of their performance. Plus, we have shortened our financial close cycle from 14 days to 6 days and financial analysts can drill from summary data to detail journal entry data with ease. Finance costs have been reduced by $50 million annually. Inventory carrying

NCR (cont'd.)

costs are lower by $10 million. Customer Services reporting cost has been cut by $3 million.

There's still work to be done, but we're on the path. We've committed the company to change and we're following through with our vision for a truly global NCR.

A vast amount of the research and analysis resources in many companies is drained in the process of searching for information, and then arguing about its validity. The average executive regularly looks at 10 to 20 different metrics. Typically the marketing department's analytics differ from the CFO's or the supply chain's analytics. Senior executives act as mediators instead of innovators. In the meantime, business opportunities are lost and performance slumps.

Why does this happen? Companies are fragmented. Their data resources are fragmented. Information is stored in separate locations around a company and jealously guarded by each "proprietor." Exercising dominion over bits of information makes people feel powerful and they don't want to lose that power. People don't see the big picture. There is no overarching goal that animates everyone. People create their own reality. Any change is resisted as a threat to power. The power isn't real. What's more, change is detrimental to the success of the company.

How can we avoid the fiefdoms people create for themselves? It starts with a strong, clear vision that brings all the disparate divisions in a company together. From vision flows culture and the structure of a foundation. Vision should be the driving force for all decisions.

A Single Version of the Truth

Commit the company to achieving a unified understanding of the business, a single version of the truth. This needs to be the foundation of leadership vision. Only then can an organization foster the collaboration and empowerment necessary to be truly global. How?

The old business solution would have been to centralize power and decision-making. That model doesn't work anymore. Old-fashioned top-down management created an environment of fear, distrust, internal dissension and grudging compliance—all enemies of corporate success. From headquarters to the front lines of customer service and the point of sale, employees make decisions that can create or destroy value. Yet this top-down style of management failed to recognize that the decisions and actions of people regardless of their position have an enormous impact on the entire organization. Corporate structure and resource allocation magnified management's tunnel vision.

Today's most successful leaders spread the power throughout the company. Success in the cutthroat global economy requires collaboration, cooperation and commitment. The pace of change in the market and the speed at which decisions must be made to maintain a competitive advantage demand a brand new decision-making model. Decision-making authority must be distributed among a diverse universe of individuals. Responsibility and accountability need to be shared more widely. Transparency and simplicity are essential.

In the airline industry, British Airways is simplifying and it's paying off.

British Airways

British Airways positions itself as one of the most stylish, full-service airlines with a global network. Therefore the company is constantly dealing with the arcane issues associated with an airline that serves customers around the world across a variety of cabin classes. Complex as the business is, CEO Rod Eddington's core principles are simplify, centralize and standardize. Determine what is useful and eliminate wasteful complexity. Having a single authoritative source for information around the company is imperative to implementing this vision.

Every division in the company is now asking itself, can this be done more effectively and efficiently? Do the different cabin

British Airways (cont'd.)

classes we offer add value? What is the optimal catering mix? What aircraft mix is best for our fleet?

One example of such complexity is British Airways' fleet of aircraft. The airline used to have multiple layers of fleets and sub-fleets and sub-sub-fleets of aircraft. The airline recognized the need for fleet simplification and the engineering division asked itself, is this complexity necessary? The answer—no. Fleet complexity was wasteful. It ran up costs and unnecessarily complicated the maintenance of aircraft types and the scheduling of engineers. British Airways has standardized its aircraft fleet, thereby reducing costs and complexity. This is just one example of Eddington's vision of simplification in action.

The leadership role is even more crucial as companies simplify, centralize and standardize, dispersing decision-making. Decentralized organizations demand clear, consistent vision disseminated by leadership's action and example. To avoid fragmentation we must strike a careful balance between encouraging and enabling decision-making by others and achieving a unified corporate vision, seamless communication, transparent operations and a universal core understanding of what differentiates the business from its competitors in the marketplace.

To manage effectively in today's information-driven market environment, executives must create a corporate culture in which creativity and the ability to manage change are fostered without losing control over core operations. Embrace productive change and demand the same of the rest of the company. Everyone in a company follows our lead. Corporate leadership is not a democracy. The core vision of a company comes from the top. The rest of the company can then be empowered to realize that vision.

> Centralize goals.
> Democratize decisions.

A unified enterprise prevents the counter-productive fragmentation of siloed divisions and promotes stability and control in concert with the flexibility necessary to compete and seize opportunities as they arise.

It seems like a paradox, but understanding the single truth of an enterprise, rather than locking leadership and the company into a status quo of behavior, enables more creative responses to business problems. Harrah's Entertainment proved this.

Harrah's Entertainment

Harrah's Entertainment leads the gaming industry in profitability. It achieved its leadership position because, from CEO Phil Satre down to the front lines of the company, Harrah's committed itself to creating a corporate culture that embraced a single integrated view of the enterprise. In order to do that effectively Harrah's had to overcome the classic gaming industry dogma that each property is a separate operation unto itself and therefore each property's business information is an asset "owned" by that single property rather than the entire corporation. Each of Harrah's casinos kept its own records. Getting a clear understanding of all the points of contact with a single customer across Harrah's many casino properties took too long to yield any business opportunity.

Harrah's suspected that customers who gambled at their Atlantic City casino probably also gambled in other cities, maybe even at a Harrah's-owned casino. But the company wasn't tapping that opportunity, because putting the information together from across the properties was too time consuming. Harrah's performance in the industry lagged.

Harrah's (cont'd.)   In 1997, Harrah's initiated the first ever cross-casino recognition and rewards program and broke down the gaming paradigm. Today, its robust rewards program, Total Rewards, allows Harrah's to see its customers' behaviors, preferences and needs no matter which property they are staying at. So the company can target incentives strategically and deliver what customers want, when they want it.

The tiered loyalty card program drives a host of service and marketing initiatives. At every point of contact, the slot machine, hotel check-in, restaurants, call centers, the Web site and everywhere else the company touches its customers, Harrah's can customize the interaction, make tailored offers and personalize service. Harrah's can now accurately predict customer response to each of its various initiatives. That means higher response rates and a more profitable relationship with the customer.

From 1997–2000, Harrah's conservative measurements show an after-tax 60 percent internal rate of return on the Total Rewards program. Taking timely advantage of opportunities has fueled enormous growth and made Harrah's an industry leader, market leadership that's only possible because Harrah's has a single version of the truth, enterprise-wide.

As Senior Vice President John Boushy says, the Holy Grail at Harrah's is to manage information *once.*

Managing from a single, complete view of the company means no surprises. Everyone hates surprises—the market most of all. It is a balancing act. The stronger the core, the more the margins can sustain, even encourage, up-to-the-minute responses to changes in the fast-paced business environment.

In the telecom industry, the speed of technological change and fickle customers mean that agility and responsiveness are prerequisites for success. To compete in the market, telecom companies must be structured to capitalize on their information.

Telephone companies traditionally organized their billing systems by telephone number. In the mid-90s Belgacom, a Belgian telecom owned 50 percent plus a share by the government and the balance by a consortium between SBC, TeleDanmark and SingTel, realized that this telephone number–based system was confusing to the customer, open to fraud and unnecessarily fragmented. The CEO called for a new customer focus and charged the company with achieving a single view of its customers. He spearheaded a corporate reorganization around customer-focused divisions—corporate, individual, small business and residential.

Now Belgacom sees all the business of each of its customers and is able to quickly analyze customer satisfaction, customer performance and the profitability of products. And the ability to better analyze brings with it more satisfied customers, higher performance and increased profitability.

Belgacom

A single view of the enterprise supports the CEO's strategic vision. Top managers and frontline employees alike must be empowered to see the global business in the same way—one set of numbers, the right numbers; one version of the truth. Strategic, tactical and event-driven decision-making requires that detail level data from across the enterprise be put in the hands of those on the front line, such things as details of customer relationships, the demand chain, the supply chain, financial operations, business process management, e-commerce and industry-specific operations are just a few examples. Speed and quality, once an either/or proposition in business decisions, are *both* equally critical now and only a company with a single view of its business can achieve both.

Managing relationships is an integrated and critical part of core business operations. Organizations previously managed by product or service, but now they manage by relationships—with customers, with partners and suppliers and with employees. Managing customers, finance, logistics, marketing and every other business function is about fostering valuable relationships. Open communication and the flow of information are the basis of good relationship management. The front office and back office become one open office. Better and faster operational decisions go hand in hand with better and faster customer communications. Companies that achieve this level of business intelligence cut costs and achieve significant improvements in their return on investment.

A successfully implemented vision requires a single version of the truth, disseminated to the company and acted on by everyone. The idea is great in theory. How is decision-making effectively dispersed in reality? The first step is to empower employees with current, comprehensive and integrated information.

Empower Employees

Success demands a clear, consistent vision of the business and its future and a robust organization to realize that potential. Empower everyone in the company to do their jobs better every day. Create a global culture of empowerment and knowledge sharing. Access to actionable information is the key to unleashing creativity and harnessing the brainpower of employees. With the right resources at their fingertips, and our support, employees *will* rise to the challenge.

> Enable a culture of proactive, solution-oriented employees, from top management to the front line, and they will unlock the value of your information resources.

Empowered people make things happen. Here's an inspiring example of frontline empowerment and quick solutions from the airline industry.

> At Gate B15 in a major airline's hub city, a flight is leaving for Boston at 7:15 p.m. Across the way at Gate B16, a flight for Hartford on the same airline is scheduled to leave at 7:10 p.m. But the Hartford-bound plane has mechanical difficulties. The traditional solution is to wait three hours for a new plane to be rerouted to the hub. But a combination of empowered employees, non-traditional thinking and cutting edge technology offers the airline a creative alternative. The Boston flight is only half full. The Hartford flight is less than half full. Rerouting the Boston flight to include a stop in Hartford will cause only a 45-minute delay in the Boston flight. It's done with minimal fuss and maximum customer management. With 15 minutes to go, the Hartford passengers are ushered across the hall to Gate B15. The Hartford passengers are delighted. The Boston passengers know it could easily have been them and they are impressed with the airline's care and concern for its customers.
>
> Only a few years ago this solution would have been unthinkable. Not because nobody thought of it. They did. The brainpower and creativity to solve the problem existed, but gate check personnel were not empowered to execute the plan. And they lacked the capacity to see all the relevant data needed to make the decision in the compressed time frame required. Now this capability exists and one airline has unlocked a wellspring of new value right at the airport counter. It has created a culture of empowerment. A culture supported by the latest technology. A culture that enables it to implement its vision of the airline of the future on the front line, at the counter, where it matters most.

Why do empowered employees make things happen? Because they ask questions and, when they get answers they can trust, they ask more questions.

A Culture of Questions

Generating the same reports over and over again will never provide fresh insight. Greater profits and productivity require creativity. They require thinking about problems in alternative ways. They demand that traditional thinking be turned on its head. Corporate culture needs to empower people to think ahead. Organizations need to be proactive, not reactive.

No matter how smart or curious people are they can't overcome the obstacle of fragmented information sources. But when the same information is made available to everyone, and it's consistent and accurate, the people asking questions will trust it. The more they trust the information, the more precise their questions will become and the less assumptions they will make. They will have the ability to accurately investigate the entire business environment in which they operate and make decisions to extract added value from it—quickly and accurately.

In order to capitalize on their information resources, companies need to ask new questions, unusual questions and penetrating questions with unknown and possibly unexpected answers. The more detailed the question, the greater the potential return. Questions answered with summary data are rarely specific enough to yield new insight. Questions answered from detail data lead to new, more detailed questions and will reveal new opportunities. Asking questions is the best way of doing business. Continental has proven it time and again.

Continental Airlines

Larry Kellner, president of Continental Airlines Inc., is regarded as a margin manager. While he focuses on costs and revenues, his mantra is margin, making more than he's spending. Like many companies, employees are one of the key resources at Continental, and more productive employees mean better margins.

Kellner believes that employees rarely make mistakes on purpose. But without the relevant data, the thousands of decisions that Continental makes about its over 2,000 flights a day would be based on guesses and assumptions. In an environment without reliable information, a person is set up to fail.

When Kellner started at Continental in 1995 there was one daily performance report, with no financial data, and historical data was inaccessible for detailed analysis. Kellner and CEO, Gordon Bethune, had a vision of a company that put all the information its people needed at their fingertips. They believed that with the right information people would not only make the right decisions, when decisions needed to be made, but would also spot new opportunities. So actionable information is a double bonus and, in Kellner's experience, employees flourish when they are given the opportunity. It's a win-win situation. Empowered employees mean better business. Motivated employees are happier and happy employees are more motivated. Continental earns accolades for every aspect of its operations *and* in 2003 the company ranked on the Fortune 100 Best Companies to Work For list for the fifth consecutive year—an accomplishment that only about 20 companies have achieved.

It's not only the employees who are asking questions. Every day Kellner has his eye on thousands of seemingly small things, asking how Continental might improve. Leadership sets the pace.

In a proactive business culture with the right tools and infrastructure in place, creative employees at every level of the organization can get answers to complex mission-critical questions in minutes, answers that might have taken days or weeks to find before—long after the opportunity was lost.

Here's another example of the power of asking questions.

METRO Group   In 1997, at METRO Group, a major international retailer based in Germany with cash and carry, food retail, nonfood retail and department store divisions, the management realized that the essential prerequisite for the successful implementation of all their business strategies is the in-depth understanding of customer needs. Only through detail information can individual customer groups be targeted and retained to the business. Only the combination of all relevant data in one system can create the common language for all important business metrics. Now, after a major information initiative, every division member receives key data such as sales, profit, stock turn, customer traffic and average basket size every day. Fine-tuning is considered the art of profitable merchandise and customer management. Which might mean that the Frankfurt cash and carry store receives a high-level call from management asking why sales are down together with headquarter analyst's suggestions on where to focus attention for improvement.

Senior management has set a high standard of asking questions and drilling down into the details of the business.

At METRO Group, management is sending an important message. Employees at every level understand that asking questions is essential and understanding the details of the business for which they are responsible is critical. With empowerment comes accountability and responsibility. With empowerment also comes higher profitability.

> If a new generation of questions
> is possible, a new generation
> of answers is enabled.

Wireless telephone companies lose in the neighborhood of 18,500 customers a day. It's called churn, and every wireless company has to deal with the challenge. The cost differential between retaining existing customers and securing new customers is approximately 1:7. It costs seven times more to acquire a new customer as it does to keep a customer. When a customer calls to cancel an account the customer service representative taking the call has less than two minutes to decide if they should try to convince the customer to stay and, if so, how best to do it. Keep in mind, the resources expended to keep that customer are one seventh of what it will cost to replace the customer. The customer representative needs fast answers to a host of questions that draw on information from around the company.

- How valuable is this customer's contract?
- What is the lifetime value?
- How well have we serviced this customer in the past?
- How many of her calls have we dropped recently?
- Which of our cross-sell offers has she responded to and what might she respond to?
- What are competitors offering?
- Can we beat their offer?

In the retail industry, Wal-Mart's ability to ask questions at every level is a model we can all learn from.

David Glass, Chairman of Wal-Mart, has information in his DNA; not surprisingly, so does Wal-Mart. Glass makes a practice of asking hard, detailed questions of his managers, every day. Why aren't shovels selling in Detroit? What else do people buy when they pick up diapers? His questions set the pace for the company. To be successful at Wal-Mart down the line, asking detailed questions and looking at the business and how to do it better are critical.

Wal-Mart

Wal-Mart (cont'd.)

In a store in Laredo, Texas, for example, the manager analyzes years' worth of sales data, factors in variables like weather and school schedules, and predicts the optimal number of cases of Gatorade, in what flavors and sizes, the store needs for the Friday before Labor Day. But that's not it. Then if the weather forecast suddenly calls for five degrees hotter, the manager has already arranged for an extra delivery of Gatorade.

At Wal-Mart, attention to detail means the company is prepared for change and able to seize opportunities on a day-by-day basis.

Asking detailed questions is valuable, on the top line and the bottom line.

These kinds of questions exist in every industry. Being able to answer questions at this level of detail has enormous implications. Corporate leaders must create a culture that encourages employees to ask the profitable questions, a culture that gives them the actionable business intelligence to do it. Regular reports are only a starting place. Daily, weekly and monthly reports are good for showing past errors but they don't lead to new ideas. Innovation requires looking to the future, asking new questions and looking at information in new ways.

Experts Say

The Devil is in the detail. Information that is captured once and at the source provides the most dynamic view of the details, as it enables companies to build upon previous knowledge, expand their current understanding of their environment, and it enables business leaders to make faster, more informed, business-impacting decisions.

Randy Mott
Senior VP/CIO
Dell

Asking questions does more than enable innovative solutions. It is a process of leveraging history to predict the future and knowing the business so well surprises don't happen. Downturns in business rarely happen out of the blue. The information is out there; it's up to us to keep track of it and heed the warning signs.

In 1997, as the Asian economic **Qantas** crisis began to unfold, Qantas had seen some early warning signs of the impending downturn as bookings from Asia to Australia began to erode.

The airline's senior management was able to adjust to what it correctly suspected was a major economic downturn in Asia by taking swift action in cancelling services and redeploying the assets to operate in more profitable markets.

Qantas' three-tier information system combines regular performance reports, "what-if" queries by business analysts who constantly remodel the reports and the ability to conduct investigative research in the data. The granularity and availability of Qantas' data enabled it to react quickly and effectively to rapidly changing business forecasts. Qantas was not caught off guard by the Asian economic crisis. Control over its information means control over the future.

Control over core operations gives us the space to innovate and to envision where the company can go next. Industry leaders achieve their position because they build a rock-solid foundation of information and analysis. Strong leadership vision, a single version of the truth and empowered employees asking questions—these are the hallmarks of a company prepared to prosper in the new economy. Successful companies shape their own future and that of their entire market. Let's see how different companies are doing it.

CONTROL

3

**Leverage
Corporate
Ecosystems**

A company is an ecosystem. Information sustains and enables the connections between the disparate members—customers, suppliers, partners and internal operations. But for many companies fragmentation has disrupted the connections. Without the free flow of information throughout an enterprise the ability to ask questions, get answers and solve problems is diminished. Opportunities are missed. Frustrated employees are less productive.

How do we structure our organizations to best capitalize on the access and use of our information resources? How do we eliminate fragmentation and optimize our opportunities? By consolidating the disparate data fragments spread throughout our various divisions and units, so that everyone who needs it has access to timely and accurate actionable information from one centralized resource, we ensure that everyone in the ecosystem has one consistent view of the business. One resource means one view.

Fragmentation and Consolidation

> Fragmentation costs money.

Consider this—a global manufacturing company with buying managers around the world has an enormous procurement budget. Without knowing it, the company's managers may be buying supplies from the same companies in different parts of the world. If they knew, they could aggregate their buying power and potentially save millions of dollars a year.

The buying managers need one view. The company needs information resources feeding its network of relationships. If the information is available, managers can act on it, and not just managers, but downstream deep into the organization employees will be better able to make daily decisions. The savings are immediate. Controlling outcomes expands opportunity.

It is of course possible to patch together the scattered information sources in a company and create makeshift links, dotted line connections. But those links will only be as strong as the question they were originally built to answer. Makeshift connections are not agile. Makeshift connections can't accommodate new ways of looking at problems. They can't instigate new questions or offer new solutions. Patches are necessarily constructed to fix an *existing* problem—they don't prepare a company for the unexpected. Retrofitting is, unfortunately, exactly what it says— backward-looking, unable to adapt to an uncertain future. No one drives by looking in the rearview mirror. Why run a business that way? Information sources linked by makeshift connections will generate mistakes like multiple, different sales offers sent to the same marketing prospect, or new loans approved for bank clients currently in default.

Patching doesn't solve fragmentation, and it doesn't save money. Information has to be truly consolidated into one centralized resource. Information is only an actionable, forward-looking resource when it delivers a complete, consistent view of the business and thus can answer any question into the future.

This may sound like a grand scale, expensive project. It's not. A strategically targeted, incremental consolidation plan will result in cost reductions right away. Start with input from users and develop a small but scalable first step. The demonstrable results will fuel the natural expansion of the project. It's simple economics. Getting rid of silos, stovepipes, divisional units—in other words, getting rid of fragmentation— always makes good financial sense. The benefits of consolidating are cost savings and revenue opportunities. Let's look at some top companies who are making the right changes. Here are just three companies across the banking, retail and package delivery industries that have proven the simple economic truth—consolidating pays off. Let's turn to the banking industry first.

Bank of America   After years of an aggressive acquisition strategy, Bank of America's information systems were an amalgam of many different companies. Prior to merger, each company had operated as its own entity. And, that meant in the wake of a decade of organizational consolidation, the state of the information resources remained scattered, inconsistent and incomplete. As Cathy Bessant, Chief Marketing Officer says, "ships passing in the night" conversations were common and time consuming as people debated over competing data, instead of honing in on solutions. Bessant said it was clear to executive management that one version of the truth is essential to improving the business. Achieving a single version of the truth became a shared goal throughout the company. Having access to one consistent set of facts significantly enhances risk management, balance sheet management, decision-making and, ultimately, the customer experience. It also means the bank can better protect the privacy of customers' information—among the highest priorities for Bank of America as foundational elements to earning trust and strengthening relationships.

Getting disparate departments to agree on the budgetary requirements of achieving the vision of a single version of the truth was complicated. Fortunately, the Bank of America team, thinking pragmatically, demonstrated that the first crucial decision could be made based on simple economics. The cost savings of having one consistent, reliable, sustainable, centralized hub for all information resources would be substantially less expensive than continuing the fragmentation—a $60 million savings over three years. In the first year alone the project was self-funding. The decision to centralize was only the first of what will be many decisions.

The project of achieving a single version of the truth is ongoing, but enormous progress has been made. Once people understood they could trust the new information capability, the demand for access to it skyrocketed. Less time is spent on the data debate. Conservative estimates are that productivity increased 20 percent. The velocity of customer contact increased, and at 150 customer contacts per second, there's no doubt that even the smallest increments of improvement in those moments are a gold mine of untapped value. With reliable data at their fingertips, frontline associates will be better able to serve the particular needs of clients in real-time, while understanding the profit implications to the bank. Not only will customer satisfaction and profitability be improved, employees will be energized. Eliminating fragmentation unleashes employee creativity and the results show up on the bottom line.

In the retail industry, here's one of the ways that Office Depot has been retooled.

Office Depot

Office Depot is one of the largest suppliers of office products to individuals and businesses. The company leads the industry in every distribution channel, including catalogue, Web, retail stores and contract services. The company bet a significant amount of its advertising budget on the idea that store customers would ultimately migrate to the Web and vice versa. Office Depot believed that customers in one distribution channel would become customers in another channel if they were offered the right incentives. The decision was based on assumptions derived from summary data from each channel, which, it turned out, was misleading when aggregated from the disparate sources.

Office Depot (cont'd.)

When the company centralized its information and was finally able to look at the details of its assumptions, this long-held principle was proven wrong. It turned out that customers who shop through a particular channel tend to stay in that channel, and not switch to another. Office Depot realized a $26 million savings in its advertising budget simply by dropping the cross-channel promotional initiatives targeted at switching customers to new channels. The money saved was redeployed to proven profitable initiatives.

In Germany, Deutsche Post is realizing the value of consolidating on the quality management front.

Deutsche Post

In 1998 German postal giant Deutsche Post's quality management was in need of improvement. There were several ways of doing things. Information source availability as well as a clear understanding and common view on the required data needed to be developed. The information on a package was kept in separate systems, so it was difficult to track the full cycle of a package delivery. This made the short-term rectification of quality issues difficult.

Deutsche Post was able to save significant resources just by consolidating its information, instead of housing information in disparate parallel locations. But the real value was realized through quality improvements made possible by the centralization of information. The ability to truly measure and manage quality issues through key performance indicators resulted in delivery time improvements in the order of 5 to 6 percent over three years, which, for the postal business, is materially significant.

Added to those improvements is the fact that with reliable information consistently available, the workplace culture has become more dynamic. Employees have changed from information seekers to information analysts. The more involved employees are, the more creative, solution-oriented and productive they become—yet another example of how processes can be optimized as well as cost savings realized.

Doing business better doesn't cost money. It earns money. Eliminate fragmentation. Centralize, standardize and make accessible the information resources in the company. It makes economic sense.

Putting Information Together

The cases above focused on the significant cost savings consolidation enables. What about the opportunities we've mentioned? Why and how are our opportunities multiplied? Our information resources enable us to see our business more accurately, make better, faster decisions and look into the future.

> Information makes no assumptions—it helps find unique associations.

Complete, consistent and freely available information that has a single version of the truth enables a company to see the business as it can be and leverage that new insight to create value. Here are just a few select examples of how companies have been profitably putting their information together.

Nationwide Insurance Until recently, anything but the simplest questions at Nationwide Insurance required IT programmers to help retrieve the necessary information. It could take months to obtain data needed for analysis, and reporting systems were only updated quarterly, which created a substantial lag between when things happened and when senior management knew about it.

It was in this environment that the president of Nationwide asked for a monthly view of early term losses (claims filed very quickly by new customers). An initiative was just getting under way to centralize and standardize information with monthly updates, and the president's request provided the first test of the project's worth.

What did the early term loss analysis show? The likelihood of claims on newer policies had increased dramatically in recent years, demonstrating a distinct deterioration in new business underwriting practices. Aggressive actions were taken to address this.

Better tracking of early term experience is only one of the many benefits of putting all the information together. Another major benefit is improvements in the pricing process. Pricing is one of the most complicated tasks in the insurance process. The centralization project has reduced the time required to perform rate reviews. Access to the same information sources as other divisions in the company eliminates questions about whose version of the truth is correct. Instead analysts can focus on more efficient and responsive sensitivity analysis. In addition to the business solutions, the centralization project has allowed the retirement of an expensive system used exclusively for pricing analyses.

Early term tracking and pricing are just two of the areas that have benefited. Across the functional areas of the company hundreds of people can access information directly now, getting answers to complex "what if" scenarios in seconds or minutes, which means better, faster decisions.

Consolidating its information resources gives Nationwide Insurance the speed and accuracy essential to compete in its industry. Fortunately, consolidation is profitable for every industry.

Whirlpool

Whirlpool, a major home appliance company, has reduced its annual warranty costs by 10 percent by putting all of its information together to better track customer complaints and identify the source of common problems with unprecedented speed and accuracy. In one instance consumers began complaining about a buzzing in a particular oven model. Whirlpool was able to aggregate the common complaints, trace them to a faulty transformer and switch suppliers with ease and efficiency.

Without centralized information the ability to respond to customers might have been delayed many months while various divisions struggled to coordinate their data and develop a consistent response. Customers were frustrated. Now, with centralization, not only are costs down, customer satisfaction is up. Just as important, overall complaints are down because faster responses mean fewer serial complaints and good information means Whirlpool can anticipate problems and deal with them proactively *before* complaints occur.

The issue in this next industry is not complaints but risk management in the financial markets.

The China Securities Depositary & Clearing Corporation Limited Shanghai Branch

The China Securities Depositary & Clearing Corporation Limited Shanghai Branch provides information to 84 securities companies and helps all its members to improve their risk management capabilities. To do this it is essential for the Exchange to have complete, up-to-date and accurate information on all the daily trading activity and have access to historical trading data for analysis.

Having a single version of the truth is the business of a stock exchange. Moving from high finance to holidays, here's a short study from the travel industry.

TUI Netherlands

One of the greater challenges facing TUI Netherlands, the largest tour company in the Netherlands, is to distinguish its offerings from other tour packagers. Customers are rarely loyal to a particular tour company. They just want to go on holiday. TUI, for example, has discovered through market research that travel customers do not respond significantly to tour operator loyalty programs. As a result, most tour packagers are product centric. Yet it is the behavior of the customers that is the most critical information for TUI to effectively and efficiently package products customers will want.

There is a second level of complexity. TUI's customers are travel agents, but the true consumers of TUI's products are the travelers. So TUI is taking a two-pronged approach to the problem. The company is working to get to know its travel agents better, focusing on the issues of importance to travel agents—speed, ease of booking and response to complaints. And it is working to get to know the end customers better. Identifying what is important to travelers—room location, size or view, flight preferences, calendar preferences, perk preferences, complaint hot buttons and style of travel. TUI plans to move to a more dynamic packaging and pricing model that is totally responsive to the consumers' desires. With better information, TUI will be able to tailor its packages more precisely, provide more information and booking capability over the Web, and reduce the load on the call centers.

TUI faces the expected resistance to a project of this scale. There are always those who "just" want to conduct the daily business and not waste time. But there is no such hesitancy at the board level. The company knows that the business of the future is connected to its customers, responsive to their needs and always dynamic.

These companies provide great examples of the power and profitability of consolidation and demonstrate the effectiveness of consolidation across industries. Every company in every industry can benefit from eliminating fragmentation.

Asking Questions

Fragmentation impairs our ability to leverage the information resources we have, because we can't use the data. Consolidation enables us to ask not only "I don't know" questions but also the even more important "what if" questions that can drive new initiatives. When we can ask questions of our information, we gain new insight into our business. When we stop making assumptions and start making decisions based on facts, we can leverage our knowledge to capitalize on opportunities.

Continental Airlines

Continental Airlines never assumes anything. In 1999 all aircraft in the United States were required to comply with a new set of higher noise restriction standards at takeoff and landing. Every airline, except Continental, hush-kitted their airplane engines. Continental got rid of all its non-compliant airplanes (Stage 2 airplanes) and replaced them with new airplanes (Stage 3 airplanes). Why? Because CEO, Gordon Bethune asked the right question.

At what price, he wanted to know, did it make more financial sense to replace a plane than to put on a hush-kit? Drilling down into the facts and data, Continental was able to determine that the benefit of standardizing its diverse airplane fleet would be cheaper than retrofitting its existing planes. On the cost side were the new airplanes. But on the return side were: savings from not investing in the patch-together solution of a hush-kit (estimated at $1.25 million per engine, it was not an insignificant cost); higher fuel efficiency; cheaper maintenance; and because of the new fleet consistency there were the additional, measurable benefits of interchangeable spare parts and crew flexibility to work any flight.

Having access to the wealth of information needed to answer Bethune's question enabled Continental to comply with federal regulation, while saving money and improving its fleet.

When other airlines were taking the view that they had "no choice" but to hush-kit their planes, Bethune's one astute question proved that assumption wrong. Bethune's philosophy, and the philosophy by which Continental is guided, is to investigate the information closely before making a decision. Ask questions and keep asking questions until the right path is clear.

Of course, Continental is not the only airline asking lots of questions now. British Airways adheres to the principle that managing its data sensibly will enable it to make better decisions.

In theory the airline industry **British Airways**
should be simple. As Paul Coby,
British Airways CIO says, "It's all about moving people from A to B." In practice, of course, there is much more to it than that. Decisions regarding price, frequency, demand, staffing and other resources must be made based on the information available. The more available the information, the better the decisions will be. British Airways realized that the key to making this a reality was to have all the data about its operations and customers in one place.

It is important that key business areas within the airline have access to information to make effective decisions. For example, the operations area may require information to such questions as what are the volumes, prices and yields on each route? Where will flight frequency increase or decrease? Crew availability? Marketing can ask about the customer experience. How was the travel and booking experience? How was flying with the airline? How frequently do the customers travel?

With all this information in one authoritative source, British Airways is enabled to ask questions about future demand and detect subtler shifts in the market. As its use of information becomes more intelligent, the better the airline can operate in today's challenging market.

Employee Value

As if eliminating fragmentation didn't already have enough benefits—saving money and solving problems—there is one more. Consolidation has a clear impact on employees. Enabling employees to ask questions and find solutions unleashes their ingenuity. Employees are happier when they are challenged and that in turn leads to better performance. Enabling employees to do their jobs better makes them feel more valued *and* makes them more valuable to the company.

Fortunately happiness has bottom-line value at two levels. The company is able to attract better employees *and* improve retention. Top performing employees will create more value. Improving retention saves resources that would otherwise have been deployed to hiring and training. When employee turnover rates are high, so are the costs associated with recruiting and bringing new hires up to speed. It turns out that eliminating fragmentation is a good investment from the employee perspective too.

Does that mean every single employee should see every bit of data and feel free to ask questions and search for solutions to any problem? No. As information becomes more accessible, information governance becomes more important. If the people who need information are going to get it how and when they need it, information can't be preorganized. To anticipate the questions people will ask as data is being collected will limit its usefulness. To be of use information needs to be freely available in flexible formats.

SBC

But as SBC CIO Ed Glotzbach points out, SBC wants more ubiquitous and intelligent use of its information resources, without providing every piece of data to every person. A balance needs to be struck that gives access to information to those who need it, without predetermining what they might need it for. The Achilles heel of centralized and available information, says Glotzbach, is the oft-held belief that everyone should have access. In practice that means people who have no reason to be spending their time asking questions are neglecting their real job responsibilities. It's analogous to the time lost to Web surfing at many companies that provide Internet access to everyone. Information can and should be empowering, but access needs to be assessed on an ongoing need-to or right-to-know basis.

So how does a corporate ecosystem, well oiled with information, actually run? In the next two chapters we'll break the issues down and look at them from the perspective of each of the three integral mini-ecosystems within every company—customers, suppliers and partners, and internal operations. Let's look at each in turn.

CONTROL

4

The
Customer
Ecosystem

Every business has customers. So the relationships companies create with their customers are critical to success. Customers come in many forms, from individuals to large corporations, but they are all similar in one way—customers *want*. No matter what the industry, today's customers have more control and expect to have more input. These new sophisticated customers look for a relationship that exceeds their expectations. A company will no longer be compared only against the best in its particular industry. Standards aren't industry-specific anymore. A company will be compared against the best in class in every industry with which their customers deal. To create the right relationship has become that much more challenging.

Gartner Inc.

Scott Nelson, a leading industry analyst at Gartner Inc., says that one of the main barriers to successful customer relationships is an unwillingness to commit to the five prerequisites of success:

- a forward-looking strategy
- the right technology
- an implementation process
- development of the appropriate skill sets
- ongoing competitive tactics

This lack of commitment, Nelson says, may be partially attributed to a general failure to have one person ultimately in charge of the issue, a "Chief Customer Officer." Ideally, this role should be synonymous with being the CEO, but it isn't. Without specific commitment to the issue, making the necessary changes is slow to happen. Consulting companies like Accenture and PriceWaterhouseCoopers are beginning to step into the breach. They understand that to have a successful relationship with its customers, a company must first commit to its employees—training, preparing and empowering them to handle the relationship.

Most large companies are still structured to be product-centric, not customer-centric, but that's changing fast. As companies become more aware of the value inherent in the customer relationship, they are refocusing the business to place more emphasis on the long-term profit potential in their customer connections. To do that, companies need to better understand their customers and deliver what customers want, when and how they want it. It's simple in concept, but requires commitment throughout an organization to execute.

Don Peppers and Martha Rogers, founders of Peppers and Rogers Group, are credited with building general understanding of one-to-one strategies. They say that to build learning relationships with customers, a company must be able to:

Peppers and Rogers Group

- **Identify** each customer at every touchpoint, and link all interaction and transaction data about each customer over time, product divisions, and geographies
- **Differentiate** each customer from every other by actual and potential value to the firm, and by the needs each customer has from the firm
- **Interact** with each customer and remember feedback to learn which customers are more valuable and what customers' needs are
- **Customize** some aspect of treatment by the company to capitalize on the feedback, and to provide a level of service no competitor can who doesn't have this customer's information

Peppers and Rogers emphasize that the difficult part for a company that uses its customer information is not so much the vision or the capabilities as the implementation—aligning a firm's processes, organization, culture, metrics, and compensation to focus on growing the value of the customer base.

Knowing what a customer wants and creating the right relationship is the bottom line. Every customer wants:

- quality and value
- to have their specific, immediate needs met
- to have their future needs anticipated
- personalized service
- to be appreciated for their business

Once the company commits itself to serving those customer wants, the relationship must be consistently sustained in every channel through which the company deals with them. Not only does a company need to have a single *internal* version of the truth, customers need to see one consistent company, too, in every channel, division or branch.

Achieving this kind of relationship is only possible if a company and its employees have access to all the information they need to deal effectively with each customer at the moment that customer orders, calls, logs on, walks into a store or in any way connects with the company through an available channel. Without this consistency, no meaningful relationship can exist.

Patricia Seybold Group Patricia Seybold, President of Patricia Seybold Group, says that global competition is about customer experience, not price wars. Every good company is asking how it can move from being product-centric to customer-centric. Globalization means companies need to focus on every stage of the relationship with a customer, from proposal to maintenance and follow-up. A company can't get a proposal half-right and keep coming back with revisions. Companies need to move away from P&Ls, incentive schemes and metrics that measure and reward based only on production and sales volumes.

Seybold says the 360-degree view is only the starting point for a company. The hard part is organizational. Companies need to put in place systems structured around types of customers, accounts and customer scenarios—to adapt its business processes to dynamically interact with customers. A company must understand what the customer *needs* to do their "job" better. This means building feedback loops to identify the right metrics to measure success. Customer experience metrics need to be integrated with customer profitability metrics.

Globalization, the Internet and the sheer volume of product choice mean that customers can change allegiances with ease. Because product differentiation is often nonexistent, customers are nomads. We need to proactively create a reason why a customer should stay with us, why a customer's loyalty will be good for the customer, not just for our bottom line.

Customer relationships are achieved one transaction at a time. Information is indispensable to shaping a satisfactory transaction. It all sounds intuitively good in theory, but putting it into practice is harder. For most companies it requires a deep cultural change.

We need to consciously add "customer impact" to all our internal decision-making processes. For example, if a company has an overburdened server and is weighing the benefits of a new one, it analyzes a list of traditional factors—cost, downtime, staff and other allocations. But the company should also analyze a variety of non-traditional factors, like the morale and efficiency of the employees in the customer service call center and the impact on them of the overburdened server. A company could, for example, develop a customer satisfaction score system, which can be used to assess the impact of the overburdened server on customer service. In short, add a customer focus to its whole decision-making process. Instead of guessing the value of the new server to its end users (the customers) the company would truly *know* its value.

Similarly, if a company designs new features for its Web site, it should conduct user experience testing. Although this initially drives costs up and increases the development time, in the long run, with its eye on the customer, a company that makes this commitment is more likely to satisfy the customers they serve.

These types of focus adjustments are examples of how a company moves the customer relationship to the center of its decision-making process. It needs to be a closed loop system of constant adjustment and assessment. In the long run, having access to a wealth of information and using that information to better understand the customer will only create sustainable value if the circle is closed. A company needs to understand its customers better, not only so it can *market to* them more effectively, but also so it can *learn from* the information in an iterative feedback process. By closing the loop on understanding its customers, companies can design products and services that anticipate customers' needs, enhance contact and predict the next best interaction. The connection with customers is not just about selling; it is a relationship in which mutual benefit is always the goal.

Dell

Dell's model—"be direct"—moves the customer relationship front and center. Dell's direct model is particularly efficient because it enables the company to work one-on-one with its customers. Whether their customer is a Fortune 100 company or a small family, Dell's goal is the same, to provide the best customer experience that it can. Leveraging information is at the core of how Dell implements its vision. As Randy Mott, senior vice president and CIO of Dell, says, no matter how good your information is, it's worthless if it provides multiple answers to every question. A closed loop of consistent, complete information is the heart of the direct model. As a result, Dell can connect with what the company *knows* its customers want, not what the company *guesses* its customers want. Of course, the business impact of leveraged information extends beyond the customer relationship. Dell drives efficiencies throughout its business—reducing inventories in its supply chain and reducing its overall operating costs.

As we'll see in the next chapter, Dell's business model shows us where we need to be if we want to stay competitive.

The cultural shift to a customer focus is naturally harder in some industries than others, but it is essential in every industry. In the financial industry, for example, banks tend to be product focused. Customer relationships are often separated by checking and deposits, mortgages, investments and credit cards. Instead of consolidating their view of the customer across all these products, financial institutions have tended to stay line-of-business focused.

A classic indicator of product line silos is different divisions competing for marketing resources. A company should be working as a team. It is working for the same customers after all. When marketing budgets are allocated by business line it means companies are still offering *products* and not offering what they should *know* their individual customers want.

Of course there are some financial companies who have been leaders in implementing customer relationship protocols, instituting the profound, organization-wide changes that need to happen. Here are two financial institutions that have made customer-facing culture and deeper relationships a priority.

Barclays

In October 1999, Barclays CEO Matt Barrett made the decision that from then on everything in the business was to start with the customer and work backward from there. He wanted Barclays to be a customer-facing company, not an organization-facing company. Now business units are optimized around Barclays' knowledge of its customers and not around profit maximization by product line. What does this mean in practice?

A traditional product-focused direct mail campaign might get a 2 percent response rate, but the more important and generally ignored statistic is the 80 percent "hostility" rate. Inadequately targeted marketing can actually damage customer relationships. Focusing the business on customers means marketing is more personal and precise. Offers are based on customers' real needs, not what is convenient for Barclays to offer. Barclays is

Barclays (cont'd.)   experimenting with connecting attitudinal data like risk appetite with behavioral data to come up with a detailed understanding of its customers.

Barclays tested, for example, a new product they called "Openplan." Instead of customers seeing their finances on a profit and loss basis, it offered customers the option to view their finances as a balance sheet. The effect of this was to place the mortgage, generally the largest single financial obligation, front and center and allow the customers to see how they needed to structure their savings and investments to account for the mortgage obligation. From national launch in April 2002 to February 2003, the result was two million new Openplan accounts. In many cases, the new account represented the conversion of an existing customer from a single product relationship to a multiple product relationship. Using the enormous amount of customer data at its disposal, Barclays was able to identify what the customers needed and deliver it.

In some cases Barclays uses specific event triggers to make more precise contacts with its customers. Sales staff gets action prompts in near real-time to their desks, with the particular offers they should be making to individual customers at that time. For example, a small business stops the direct debit for its insurance payments. Is the customer thinking of changing its insurance? Barclays calls them, finds out why and offers them insurance products better suited to their needs.

The goal is always to optimize the customer experience. The result is more business for Barclays.

In the United States, Bank of America, though the third largest bank in the country, is determined to succeed with a small-bank approach to relationships.

Bank of America often gets letters **Bank of America**
from satisfied customers. But that's
not enough for the bank. Not content to rest on its laurels, the company wants to become even more relevant to its customers. Bank of America's goal is to become *the* financial advisor to its customers. To do this, it needs to deepen its relationships. The company believes that it has only begun to scratch the surface of the opportunity.

Already the company has sharpened its marketing skills, analyzing its centralized information resources to enable the bank to fully understand a customer's needs, while equipping customer service representatives to present personalized, relevant solutions to meet specific needs. Where it used to take 60 days to see results of a marketing campaign, the bank can now track results on a weekly, even daily, basis and recalibrate quickly based on responses. And almost more importantly, the company can be sure that the same marketing campaign is focused and not inconsistently touching the same customer at different times.

Deepening the customer relationship means showing customers, through targeted marketing efforts, that the company knows them and is responsive to their needs.

In every industry, what's preventing many of us from making the investment necessary to achieve a single view of the business and shift focus to the customer relationship is the size and scope of the undertaking. Fortunately, it's not an all or nothing proposition. Establishing the vision and setting the new strategy occurs over time. Where we start—what the catalyst is for change—can happen in any number of places in the company.

Gartner Inc.

Kim Collins, a leading industry analyst with Gartner Inc., talks about an array of customer metrics a company needs to be tracking to measure the benefits of implementing a customer-centric business focus. At minimum a company should be looking at the following:

Customer Satisfaction

1. Ratings
2. Complaints
3. Time to resolve issues
4. Response times

Economics

5. Cost per sale
6. Cost to service
7. Marketing expenditures

Market Share

8. Market penetration
9. Breadth of wallet
10. Value of products sold

Customer Loyalty

11. Attrition
12. Length of relationship

Customer Profitability

13. Percentage of profitable customers
14. Percentage of high-value customers
15. Lifetime value of customer base

Marketing Campaigns

16. Response rates

17. Closed sales

18. Percentage of profitable sales

Market Metrics

19. Market value and earning per share

Tracking metrics is essential to success. Only then can a company really see what's working and what's not on a timely basis and adjust its strategy accordingly. A company that tracks its metrics is better managed.

Most companies are doing "enough." They get by. Margins may flatten year to year, but the status quo is maintained. Why change? Past performance is no guarantee of future success. A self-satisfied company doesn't evolve. A commitment to continuous improvement is the only way to succeed in the long run. The job of changing will never be "done." Successful change is *necessarily* an ongoing project of fine-tuning— measuring existing initiatives, discarding unprofitable strategies and testing new projects. That's what keeps our jobs interesting as leaders in today's market.

> Long-term success comes from picking key initiatives, pushing them through specific channels, building on that momentum and spreading the "word" outward. There is no end point.

Where can we start with the seemingly overwhelming task of shifting focus to the relationship with the customer? It starts with looking at these four key aspects of the relationship. The emphasis depends on the industry, but each is ultimately critical to success:

- Acquisition—identifying and attracting new customers
- Communication—communicating effectively with prospective and existing customers
- Retention—identifying and retaining the best customers
- Profitability—increasing wallet share, customer profitability and lifetime value

The ultimate measure of success is retaining profitable customers. We'll look at each of the four components to that success in turn.

Acquisition

Winning new customers is not only about "how many." It is also about acquiring the *right* customers, the most profitable customers. Wireless phone companies, for example, have many strategies for landing new business. One is to buy information on credit-worthiness and target people with weak credit histories for prepaid wireless service, carefully targeting the right type for the particular product.

Customer acquisition is one of the most difficult strategies for increasing value. We usually have very little information on prospective customers, compared with the wealth of information we should all have by now about our existing customers—their preferences, habits and needs. The information we rely on to acquire customers is usually summary in nature—demographics and psychographics—without specifics of individual behavior. In fact, the rule of thumb in many industries is that it costs as much as seven times more to acquire a new customer than it costs to sell additional products or services to an existing customer. Being relevant to the customer is critical.

Travelocity was born on the Web. **Travelocity**
It never sees its customers in person,
and yet in many cases it knows a lot more about a customer than
many brick-and-mortar businesses. Travelocity knows its
customers. They know what their customers shop for, what
products they purchase, how often they purchase and what their
travel interests are. If a customer shops for flights to a specific
destination three times within a five-day period but does not
purchase, this might trigger a targeted travel offer for that
destination of interest. How many other companies can or do act
on a prospective customer's browsing habits? It pays off.

The more information we have, the deeper our understanding of prospective customers' wants.

It is not only about knowing our own customers and business. To craft an appropriate, unique and effective customer relationship strategy requires that we maintain a sharp eye on new market developments. We need to anticipate our competitors. Whether we are acquiring new customers, communicating with existing customers, fighting to retain them or trying to increase wallet share, knowing what products or services competitors are offering and will be offering in the future is yet another important piece of information.

Extracting the trends in customer behavior and market developments is essential to understanding any industry.

At SBC allowable information **SBC**
resources are used to spot trends
in three customer areas:

- **Demographics.** Who uses SBC's services? What is the likelihood they will buy more? What is the churn rate?
- **Volume.** What new products are appropriate given the current trends in volume and market direction?

- **Use.** What is the impact on the network? How can SBC design, engineer and provision the network for the future? What will the market want?

  The goal is not only to increase customer use but also to make the customer's experience more pleasing.

The more information we have, the better we can communicate with customers. And communication is, after all, the foundation of any relationship.

Communication

> A communication strategy is a dialogue with the customer, *not* a monologue.

How we communicate with customers and prospects is their leading indicator about what kind of company we are. A communication strategy has two goals: to move a customer to where they want to be *and* to where we want them to be. The customer wants the best products and service possible. A company wants the most profitable customer possible. These goals are not incompatible, but to match them up requires a carefully focused communication strategy.

Marketing for the sake of marketing is not a customer relationship strategy. It is a monologue without benefit of a captive audience. It is not relationship-building if every contact with a customer is an up-sell or cross-sell. Pummeling customers with "special offers" is likely to result in annoyed customers. Using customer information proactively means approaching customers with what they really want and servicing their genuine needs. Creating a profitable customer relationship requires a dialogue. That means understanding the customer and only marketing the appropriate products and services to them.

There are three fundamental questions at the core of determining the appropriate communication strategy.

- Who?
- What about?
- How often?

To answer those three questions intelligently requires information from sources around the company. These could include:

- Current products or services used
- Channel of entry or initial contact
- Marketing campaigns received
- Product information requests
- Most recent browsing history
- Current and previous sales contacts
- Prior fulfillment history
- Product returns (and for what reason)
- Pending orders
- Stock and fulfillment issues on all products
- Knowing a customer's particular pain points and satisfaction triggers

Communication and coordination among divisions and channels in a company is a prerequisite to developing and implementing an effective communication strategy with a customer.

We need to remember that communication is always marketing in some sense, but that doesn't mean it's always about a sale. Sometimes communication is about service. It's about fostering the relationship. It's still about value in the long run.

Here's just one suggestion for a profitable communication strategy. A traditional banking customer completes her first ATM transaction, a deposit. Unprompted, the bank calls to assure the customer that the transaction was successful, providing the necessary comfort level to ensure that the customer will convert to the less expensive ATM channel permanently. The customer has suddenly become far more profitable for the bank and is still satisfied with the service.

> One leading bank in the United States is able, with a detailed customer tracking system, to identify the difference between a customer who is abusing overdraft privileges and one who simply doesn't realize that a check is overdrawn.
>
> In one instance, when the bank called its customer to verify that indeed they didn't know they had insufficient funds, the customer covered the amount later the same day. The customer was able to call the person who had received the check and let them know that it could be redeposited immediately. Neither the customer nor the recipient of the check was charged any penalty. The recipient was impressed enough to become a new bank customer. They, too, wanted the personal service and attention to detail that the bank was able to offer.
>
> This top bank not only has the infrastructure needed to put the right information in the right hands. It trained its people to act on that information—one important reason why it's an industry leader.

The airline industry often provides examples of miscommunication resulting in inferior service. We've all become familiar with the litany of excuses for airline delays. What is most frustrating to customers is not the delay itself but the array of excuses often offered for the same delay. The gate staff says it's a parts problem. The counter staff says it's a plane that hasn't arrived. The pilot, once the customer gets on the plane, says it was a delay to wait for connecting passengers. What's going on? Do they simply not know the real reason? Is the beleaguered staff just trying to get irate customers off its back? In most cases it is probably a combination.

Information silos and unconnected systems mean that pockets of knowledge will develop over time, but the whole story is rarely available to everyone at the same time.

Airlines are getting smarter. They know that customers value a straight answer and reward it with loyalty. Look at what Delta Air Lines is doing with that knowledge.

Delta Air Lines

In the 11 largest airports where Delta Air Lines operates, it has installed eye-catching new flat plasma displays, known as the Gate Information Display System (GIDS) screens. These screens answer the 20 questions most frequently asked by customers. For example:

- Flight status, departure and arrival times, mileage between cities
- Destination weather and a four-day forecast
- Aircraft seating configuration
- Waiting lists for standby and upgrade passengers
- Connection information
- Boarding status, listing what rows are currently boarding
- Meal service in each cabin
- Delay, cancellation and gate change information

Delta's customers feel more respected. The company has a unified view of all the information it holds. This single version of the truth is on display for everyone to see—where it counts most.

Marketing Smart

The bulk of communication between companies and customers though is marketing for the purposes of making a specific sale. The goal of sales marketing is higher response or "take" rates and lower costs, and we shouldn't forget the often-ignored statistic, lower hostility rates. Targeting more effectively is essential, and information is the fundamental ingredient in an effective strategy.

> Actionable Information + Targeted Marketing Communication
> = Higher Take Rates + Lower Costs + Lower Hostility Rates
> = Increased Value

There really is no "junk mail." There is only misdirected marketing. In the United States, companies spend in aggregate approximately $1,800 per person, per year, on marketing campaigns. Most of those dollars are spent on marketing developed using basic analytical tools, insufficient information and barely targeted mailing, e-mail and telemarketing lists. The volume of direct mail and e-mail a typical person gets each day is a classic example of grossly misdirected marketing—catalogues the recipient will never order from, offers for seminars, credit cards and magazines they will never respond to, discount coupons for products they will never purchase.

We need to be relevant to the customer when we service them *and* when we sell to them. And, despite our earlier cautions, an educated, targeted cross-sell *can* play an important role in building the customer relationship.

Here's how different companies are marketing smart.

Sears

Sears has 120 million customers and some of the richest information resources at its disposal. Sears knows, for example, that nearly 40 percent of all major appliance purchases in the United States are made at Sears. The company knows details about those purchasers like life stage, income and home ownership. How does it use the information?

Sears recently acquired Land's End. One current initiative leverages the strong similarities between the profile of the appliance shopper, painstakingly developed over years of business, and the profile of the Land's End shopper. Targeted mailings and in-store promotions are calculated to inform customers of the new line of Land's End clothing in Sears stores. Sears is strategically serving its customers better.

Sears knows that direct mail can be a powerful marketing tool, when used well. Of course the publishing industry has long been a source of innovation in the direct mail field.

Meredith Corporation is a leading U.S. media company, focusing on

Meredith Corporation

magazine and book publishing. Their leading magazine brands include *Better Homes and Gardens* and *Ladies' Home Journal*. With information on over 70 million consumers, Meredith considers its information resources to be one of their key corporate assets and getting the highest value from the asset is a top priority. Meredith's marketing mantra is "to be there when they want us and not when they don't." To do that successfully, Meredith has to have a consistent, accurate view of each of those 70 million people. That's Meredith's goal.

Subscriber acquisition, reduced marketing costs, increased wallet share and improved revenue from list rentals are the bottom-line benefits Meredith hopes to achieve with this single view. On each of those fronts, what will better information enable?

Subscriber acquisition

- Better targeted list pulls and faster turnaround time on list pulls
- Improved subscription and renewal rates via the online channel

Reduced marketing costs

- Lowered cost of outsourcing consumer database and generating marketing lists
- Faster time to develop higher quality targeted candidate acquisition lists
- Use of Web to drive renewals

Meredith Corporation (cont'd.)

Increased wallet share

- A holistic view of consumers, channels and products
- Personalization on the Web
- Using the Web to cross-sell and up-sell

Improved revenue from list rentals

- Better targeted rental list pulls
- Identification of new subscribers and recency factor leverage

While there is still much value to be mined from its information resources, Meredith already does some of the most sophisticated and effective direct marketing in the publishing business, a business that traditionally relies heavily on direct marketing to acquire customers.

Meredith has, for example, moved aggressively into the online channel, something many brick-and-mortar companies have not been able to do successfully. The company often tests marketing campaigns online before sending out the same campaign by mail. In Meredith's experience the conversion rates from e-mail and mail campaigns are often quite similar and the e-mail campaign is an accurate bellwether for mail campaign plans.

Marketing that better understands who each customer is will be more successful. Meredith is putting their information resources to work for their bottom line.

We're seeing it over and over again: information unlocks the potential of relationships. The companies who delve into their information can create more intimate relationships.

Travelocity identifies unique customer records on their data warehouse. If a customer has multiple accounts with Travelocity, information is combined to create a single view of the customer. For example, if a customer has a business, personal and family account, Travelocity will link the accounts using a combination of data elements, including customer name, address, e-mail address and consumer link. Travelocity's focus is on having a comprehensive understanding of their customers in order to provide the most relevant communications possible, thereby driving value and strong customer relationships.

Travelocity

Like online companies, catalogue companies must personalize their relationship with the customer at a distance.

Senshukai Co. is a leading catalogue house in Japan, specializing in mail order service, shopping-center style. With over 7 million customers and 22 different catalogues, getting the right catalogue to the right customer at the right time is essential. Increasing customer responsiveness is the bottom-line goal. Understanding its customers is the core of Senshukai's business model.

Senshukai Co.

The company knows, for example, that women living in cities tend to purchase daily necessities and miscellaneous goods from catalogues, whereas women living in rural areas have a greater tendency to buy fashion goods and clothing. Based on the wealth of information the company has collected on its customers, Senshukai is able to target its mailings, taking into account a host of individual characteristics of each customer, including lifestyle, life stage, location, profession and history of shopping.

Retention

Companies acquire and communicate with customers for one specific reason—they want to retain their business. Most companies have no idea when they lose a customer—or why. They might guess at the "why," but few have the time and resources to put in the effort required to grapple with the issue effectively, identify the event that caused the loss and contact customers about it. The companies that achieve this level of contact with their customers dominate their markets.

The wireless industry, for example, is notorious for its rate of churn. Getting a handle on customer retention can put a wireless company in the top ranks of its industry. But understanding the reasons for churn is only half the battle. Acting on the information is even more critical because the rate of information atrophy is startling, not only in the telecom industry, but every industry.

The customer retention battle is event-driven and requires quick and precise responses. Imagine a trigger event, for example, canceling a wireless account. If the wireless company wants to change its customer's decision it needs to make that contact within 24 hours. Approximately 75 percent of all positive responses to customer retention calls result from calls made within the first 24 hours after the trigger event. Three-quarters of all the customers who can be influenced will be influenced in the first 24 hours after they cancel the account. After 48 hours it's often not worth even making the contact.

Making contact with a customer as close to an event as possible is the key to retention. Many of the banks you'll see in these pages have, for example, built business rules that generate action prompts following specific trigger events on an account. The action prompts are followed up within the day.

Another retention approach favored by many companies is loyalty or rewards programs calculated to bind customers more closely to the company. Rewards programs traditionally have mixed results. It's not enough to simply offer customers the chance to accumulate points and redeem them for product or flights or other services. The most successful loyalty programs use the information acquired through administering the program to actually enhance the relationship with customers.

Harrah's customer loyalty program

Harrah's

and tiered loyalty card enable it to keep very close track of its customers and precisely tailor its contacts with each customer to ensure the most benefit for both. Customers use the cards in slot machines where they are recognized and can trigger service experiences immediately. For example, Harrah's staff may approach a customer who has earned a free restaurant meal with the offer, while they are still playing the slot machine on which they earned the reward.

When a loyalty customer checks into the hotel, desk staff can see the Total Rewards information and act accordingly. They might see a customer prefers a non-smoking room, the *Wall Street Journal* at 7 a.m., or two queen beds instead of a king bed. They might see that a customer has earned cash to play or a free night at the hotel. With this knowledge at their fingertips, desk staff can personalize the service to the customer. Kiosks stationed around the gaming floor provide instant updates and information to customers about rewards earned and comps they can redeem right away. Unlike many other reward programs, Harrah's acts immediately on a customer's earned rewards and makes it simple for customers to redeem.

Retention issues take on a special twist in the retail industry where it's often impossible to know for sure why a customer abandoned a store. In the online setting, a retailer can trace a customer's behavior with more accuracy and analyze the cause of departure. In the store setting, the information that went into a customer's decision to leave simply isn't available to analyze. But a store can identify in-store situations, which may be contributing to retention issues.

Lowe's

Steven Stone, Vice President of Lowe's, a company emerging as one of the strongest competitors in its industry, knows that nothing upsets customers more than seeing long check-out lines and a bank of 25 cashier stations with only two open. Sensitive to customers' attitudes and perceptions, Lowe's used the wealth of detailed information it always has at its fingertips to determine the optimal number of stations in each store. It analyzed store traffic, speed of check-out, line lengths, average numbers of products per purchaser and a host of other details. The result— $7 million worth of cashier stations were removed from Lowe's stores without any negative impact on customer service. In fact, customer perception of service is improved, as they no longer feel frustrated by the negative image of unused stations.

Profitability

We have to protect the investment we make in acquiring and communicating with customers. We create the customer relationship with retention in mind, of course. But retaining customers is not an end in itself. Not all customers are equal. Not all customers are a good investment. The object, the source of any financial success, is retaining *profitable* customers. A loyal customer is an annuity. That doesn't mean customer relationships can be allowed to become static. Increasing wallet share and moving customers up the value chain is the most sustainable growth path for a company.

Every encounter with a customer represents an enterprise-wide opportunity to understand the customer's needs better. Acting on the opportunity means increasing wallet share. Every division and every employee is working toward one goal—improving the relationship with the customer so that customer is more profitable for the company over the long term.

For some companies, internal growth is the only possibility for expansion. In the banking industry, for example, many institutions have reached the legal limit for growth by acquisition, so their focus has by necessity shifted back to internal growth and strengthening their bonds with existing customers. Every customer counts when internal growth is the focus.

Strengthening relationships with existing customers is an imperative for companies like Royal Bank of Canada (RBC), especially when consumers today have more choices than ever before in terms of how they want to manage their finances and with whom. By using the "get to know your client" rule in creative and strategic ways, RBC is delivering integrated business and marketing plans to grow and maintain a satisfied and profitable client base.

In 1987, RBC was a traditional personal and commercial bank. It **RBC** had no trust capability, no investment banking, no wealth management, no brokerage, asset management or insurance. The bank set a target of creating a universal financial enterprise with services delivered to the customer in an integrated way. RBC is now Canada's largest bank and global financial services organization. The ultimate goal is a profitable relationship with every customer.

In practice this means three things. First, the customer experience needs to be precisely tailored. Give each individual customer "the right stuff." Customers want to be understood. They want their needs to be anticipated and their business valued. Second, the cost structure needs to be appropriate to the customer. Finally, the risk profile of each customer needs to be known and reflected in the cost structure.

RBC (cont'd.)

Any effort to tailor the customer experience must take their needs as the baseline and work through the cost structure and risk profile. 24/7 call centers and branches on every corner are not enough anymore. RBC has developed a combination of strategic and tactical segmentation codes to allow it to tailor its customers' experience. It has indicators for profitability, life cycle segment, lifetime value (five years), credit risk, vulnerability (susceptibility to leave), channel preference, commitment (loyalty) and consolidation (propensity to consolidate financial services with RBC). It has developed strategies to retain the customer, reduce their risk or grow their business.

One of the most efficient ways to serve customers is through package services that offer value for the customer and enhance profitability for the bank. It is more cost-effective for the bank and, in RBC's experience, the customer is more satisfied because they are no longer "nickeled and dimed" for every transaction, which made reading bank statements a confusing, often frustrating task. Instead customers feel their needs are understood, which is certainly something they value.

From 1999 to 2002, approximately 55 percent of RBC's personal deposit account customers were in a banking package. In 2002, 74 percent were in packages. Using the wealth of customer information at its disposal, and the detailed analytical segmentation RBC has built, the bank was able to better target its packages to the "right" customers to better meet their banking needs.

RBC's personal banking packages originally did not include Internet service. By introducing online banking as part of these packages, customers not only received greater value but were also introduced to paying many of their bills online. Today, the Internet is the most popular method used by RBC's customers to pay their bills, followed by branch, telephone and banking machine.

In the three-year period between 1999 and 2002, RBC's total number of most profitable customers rose 18 percent, or 1.2 million. Those customers' average profitability went up $80 per customer.

The first step toward internal growth to drive improved profitability is consolidating the company's understanding of its customers, achieving that critical single view of the total customer base. In an ideal company a customer's information moves "with them" as they touch the company from different angles and through varied channels. A customer should always be talking to the whole enterprise. There should be no disconnection between a customer's purchases on the Internet, calls to customer service and in-store visits. A solid communication strategy is key to growth.

Profitable customers help companies grow. We need to know how to identify them, to understand each customer's profitability.

Summary data is misleading at best and significantly flawed at worst. To rely on anything but the detailed information about an individual customer will result in poor assumptions, an inferior customer relationship and decreased customer value.

> It is simply not possible
> to maximize a customer's profitability
> based on summary and
> assumption-based information.
> Detailed, integrated data
> is the differentiator of success.

Understanding the profitability profile of customers is an essential ingredient in success.

RBC

RBC once relied on summary data to estimate the profitability of its customers. The goal was to align the right resources against the customer based on their needs and business with the bank. Then the bank made a commitment to the future by investing time and money to create an information center that consolidated all its detailed information about customers in one place. For the first time, the bank had a single, comprehensive view of each customer. To its surprise, the bank discovered that 75 percent of its customers shifted two or more profitability deciles. Customers the bank had been treating alike were, in fact, dramatically different in their banking profiles.

Customer profitability is not only a historical fact. Every customer also has an intrinsic value: a discounted present value based on future cash flows—a *lifetime value.*

RBC knows that it's critically important to differentiate between the current and potential value of clients, both in the short term and the long term. This enables the bank to serve each client better by providing the right service at the right time in the client's life stage. For example, RBC recognizes the long-term value and the future profitability potential of supporting students now, and provides such features as interest-only payments on student credit lines and higher limits for students enrolled in professional programs.

RBC

Lifetime value is the longer term view of customer profitability. We run our businesses for the long run and we should structure and prepare our organizations for that future. We should create our customer relationships for the long run too. Our strategies for acquisition, communication, retention and growth ought to be robust enough for the future. We need to align our resources in a manner that is appropriate to our customers' needs and their business with the bank. Over the long term, their lifetime value is the key to success.

CONTROL

5

Supplier, Partner and Operational Logistics

As we move to a more customer-focused business model, we need to be mindful of the two other key mini-ecosystems within the company—supplier and partner logistics and internal operations.

Supply Chain Logistics

Globalization, the high pace of market change and the explosion of information resources have ushered in a new era of collaboration. Businesses used to operate as separate entities. Globalization has broken down the vertical integration that used to be the hallmark of successful companies. In the days of Henry Ford, the car company made the steel for its cars. Ford Motor Company's Rouge River factory covered more than a thousand acres and included a steel mill, a power plant, glass and cement factories and an assembly plant. Ford's only important suppliers were coal, iron ore and sand companies. Hearst owned pulp and paper mills. NCR made the screws for its mechanical cash registers.

The Japanese dubbed these vertically integrated behemoths, *keiretsus*. Horizontal cooperation between disparate parties in the marketplace was an anomaly. That's changed. Now it's a necessity. Vertical integration is a relic. The supply chain has dissolved into a series of inter-company relationships. Companies that continue to control the supply chain end-to-end have lost their competitive advantage and will fail, unless they operate in a very specific niche with a small, sophisticated customer base.

Meta Group Dale Kutnick, CEO of Meta Group, believes that partnerships, collaboration and information sharing constitute the road to success in the future. The companies that use information well are the ones that will do well. This externalization of information, as Kutnick calls it, has created 21st century keiretsus—loose associations of autonomous companies in the supply chain.

The new information transparency brings suppliers, partners and customers into the process. Point of sale data allows suppliers to do their own resupplying. Combinatorial innovation (assembling "old" ideas in a compelling new way), which is responsible for the bulk of business success today, is made possible between partners. Overall operational efficiency is enhanced.

Kutnick defines these new companies, members of the new keiretsus, as those who make less than 30 percent of the components that are necessary to their products or services.

He gives Dell as a textbook example of a company that has capitalized on information sharing in this newly fragmented global economy.

- Dell manufactures nothing.
- It assembles parts from an array of suppliers into computers.
- It then sells directly to consumers.
- It has reduced its "inventory turn" on PCs from the traditional five to seven weeks of most computer companies to five to seven days.
- It is so wired in to its suppliers and customers that it does not order a part (a disk drive, a modem, etc.) until the equipment into which the part will be integrated is already sold.

Kutnick warns that there are three pitfalls to watch for in the new keiretsus.

1. Dependency on and quality control of business partners
2. A tendency to rely too much on too little information
3. The complexity of managing a network of disconnected business components

Bearing in mind the risks Kutnick points out, we need to rise to the market imperative, which demands broad-based collaboration and increased specialization. Managing in the new horizontal structure requires a new skill set.

> Managing complexity will
> be *the* issue facing CEOs.

Bob Parker, AMR Research Inc.   Bob Parker, Vice President of Enterprise Commerce Management Strategies at AMR Research Inc., calls this new collaborative market imperative the "economy of scope" advantage. It once was that the economies of scale inherent in verticalization were the key to corporate success. The Ford's and Hearst's were the models to follow. No longer. The days of mass marketing, automatic branding because of size and the inevitable focus on product value are over.

We are now, says Parker, in a market where microscale and the advantages of scope inherent in horizontal cooperation between companies determine success. Companies with a broad reach through established partnerships and supplier relationships and an intense specialization will be the successes of the future.

Parker pinpoints three issues facing these broadly allied companies in this time of intense global competition.

1. The need to leverage intangibles:
   a. Supplier relationships
   b. Customer relationships
   c. Intellectual property

2. Supply chain issues:

    a. **Postponement.** How can we offer more customized products and delay final packaging to the last moment?

    b. **Capitalizing on product platforms.** How can we build new products using existing value? Can we use, for example, the same drive train in the different cars that appeal to 40-year-old men and 25-year-old women?

3. Cash flow:

    a. As investors look less at earnings per share and more at cash flow per share, how can we increase the net cash the company is generating?

The key to resolving these three issues (and the crux of managing successfully in a horizontal structure of loose inter-corporate associations) is the single specific focus that drives everything a company does. Vision.

The breakdown of vertical structure has allowed companies to become more agile in a market that demands speed of response. But the fragmentation that can occur in large, siloed vertical companies is not necessarily solved. Inter-corporate associations can be equally fragmented, if each individual company does not drive its particular vision deep into its own organization and focus on its business. The balance is to extract the value of the new horizontal structure without falling prey to its pitfalls.

Information is the indispensable factor in the equation—access to information and the ability to act quickly. Timely data enables a company to act quickly on small windows of opportunity. The logistics, supply chain and pricing strategy of a business must be capable of turning on a dime. A nimble company is a successful company.

Wal-Mart

Wal-Mart is one of the most successful and agile retailers in the world today. It's not because the company has the best customer service, although of course its customer orientation is good. It's because Wal-Mart is one of the best supply-chain managers around. The company has relentlessly squeezed costs out of the supply process. Wal-Mart has achieved a previously unseen level of operational efficiency. Why? Through its Retail Link system, the company captures all sales information within short intervals. It knows exactly what's happening throughout the company at all times. Not only is Wal-Mart agile and responsive to opportunities as they arise, but it provides the key information to its suppliers, so they too can respond quickly.

Vendors like Proctor & Gamble can track sales and proactively resupply, thereby avoiding stock-outs.

Take, for example, the days following September 11, 2001. The demand for American flags in Wal-Mart stores rose from approximately 6,400 on September 11, 2000 to 116,000 on the same day in 2001. On Wednesday, September 12, 2001, the demand was 200,000 flags. In hindsight, the increased demand for flags seems obvious. At the time, it was Wal-Mart's superior information and its transparency with suppliers that enabled it to react early to order re-stocks of flags. The speed of Wal-Mart's response time allowed it to respond quickly and service an important need better than its competitors.

The relationship with suppliers and the ability to respond quickly to changes in demand, as Wal-Mart has mastered, are just one aspect of the supply chain.

Procurement is another key decision-making point in the supply chain structure. Actionable information is essential. The potential for cost efficiency in procurement can dramatically increase the return on investment of a company. A single good procurement decision can save millions of dollars. In a well-functioning information ecosystem, a company can identify suppliers globally and aggregate procurement to secure the best deal on a worldwide basis.

But procurement decisions are not strictly information based.

> Wayne Eckerson, Director of **TDWI** Education and Research at The Data Warehousing Institute,TDWI, cautions that in the general rush to the Internet as the hottest new business tool, companies should be wary of regarding business-to-business (B2B) exchanges as a panacea to procurement problems. A few years ago an online auction-style procurement system was established for global companies. The system created a network of B2B exchanges intended to create a bidding process for procurement. Of course the object was procurement efficiency. The system failed miserably. Why?
>
> The system did not take into account the complexity of procurement and the level of trust that companies have come to expect in their supplier relationships. It turned out that electronic trust could not be built in a day. Companies preferred the relationships they built one-on-one over a period of time.

That's not to say there are no gains to be realized in procurement processes. Simply that they are currently made within the ongoing relationships companies form with their suppliers.

To build trust in relationships with partners and suppliers in any aspect of supply chain management requires transparency. Transparency means an accurate and timely exchange of information between parties, so that everyone is on the same page, working from the same information. Open communication builds trust. Trust is the foundation for optimizing decision-making.

Here's one example:

METRO Group In a drive to better manage its supply chain, METRO Group has created supplier scorecards. Sales, profits, market share trends, promotion contributions, on-time deliveries, returns and defects, and incomplete orders are all weighed in to the supplier score. With this high level of detailed information at its fingertips, METRO Group can conduct better supplier negotiations and give preference to suppliers with high margins and high sales volumes. The company works with suppliers to improve co-marketing results, reduce revenue loss from out-of-stocks and reduce markdown losses from overstocks. Both parties benefit from the transparency of the information flow, building valuable trust. Workflow-based category management functions are being developed and will support users in their category decision processes.

Most recently, METRO Group has integrated suppliers into the demand planning process via CPFR (collaborative planning, forecasting and replenishment). Sales data across several years form the common basis for demand forecasting in cooperation with the suppliers.

The more transparency and trust a company can achieve between its business and its suppliers, the more efficient they all are.

The benefits of agility don't apply only to retailers and their partners up and down the supply chain. Every company benefits from being flexible and responsive. The techniques of using information to react quickly to product demand and procurement issues can be applied in a range of other business situations.

For example, Harrah's has a program that enables it to visualize the activity on the slot floor. Using color coding, a map of the slot floor shows a gradation of red through blue to indicate "hot" machines and "cold" machines. The program allows Harrah's to track the activity around hot machines, to conduct a market basket analysis, to determine the best layout of the slot machines and to provide better service to higher worth customers. Harrah's plan is to have the program running in real-time in 2003. With this level of detailed information at its disposal, Harrah's can ensure that the right product is in the right place at the right time to optimize customer satisfaction and use.

Harrah's

The horizontal relationships between companies are more important than ever. Information and information technology that enables the necessary connections provide the framework for the required trust between members of the 21st century keiretsus.

> Information and trust are the fundamental basis of every profitable relationship.

Building relationships and fostering information transparency in the supply chain, with customers, suppliers and partners, is only half the profitability equation. Internal transparency is the critical other half. Controlling operational logistics and fraud prevention is vital to managing profitability. Transparency and full information flow is essential.

Operational Logistics

Internal operational logistics are at least as complex as the external logistics of supply chain management and require as much information. Information is, for example, a baseline necessity in the package delivery business.

FedEx

For FedEx, logistics is their business. Fortunately the company has information in its DNA. The company goal is to have the information about every shipment available as nearly as possible in real-time. At FedEx there's no such thing as too much information.

A FedEx package is scanned an average of 12 times between pickup (or drop-off) and delivery:

- at pickup
- at the origin station
- on leaving the origin station
- at the airport on ramp
- at loading on the aircraft
- at off-loading from the aircraft
- at loading onto an outbound container at the hub
- on arrival at the destination ramp
- on leaving the destination ramp
- on arrival at the destination station
- at loading onto the delivery van
- at delivery

FedEx operates under the guiding principle that it can't manage what it can't measure. At every one of those scanning points, FedEx can break down the actual performance and measure it against expected results.

The operational logistics of the airline business are equally complex.

> Denis Adams, CEO of the new **Australian Airlines** Australian Airlines, a subsidiary owned 100 percent by Qantas, was collecting information on pricing, revenue management and schedules *before* the airline even flew its first route. Adams knows that the real value of the data the airline collects is in tracking the booking trends, even at an early stage.
>
> For example, before the airline officially started flying, Adams noticed a directional imbalance on the Hong Kong flights. People were booked to join Australian Airlines service *from* Southern China, but they were not using it in the opposite direction, to fly *to* Southern China. Adams knew that the sales team needed to work with travel wholesalers to provide incentives to them to fill the northbound routes, so the aircraft could profitably fly to China to pick up the southbound passengers.
>
> On other occasions, it's important to take a detailed second look at the overbooking profile on a flight. Understanding the particular characteristics of different flights is essential to setting an appropriate overbooking allowance. For example, when there are group bookings the overbooking allowance might need to be changed to reflect the risk that a group no-show will occur. The risk of a group not showing up for a flight is significantly different quantitatively than the risk of a selection of individuals not showing up. So it's crucial to drill down to the detailed information and identify the precise nature of a flight's bookings.

The key in any logistics puzzle is to look outside the standard reporting process to spot unusual trends.

The better the leaders of a company understand its *whole* business, the smoother operations will be. Here's an example from the restaurant business, where allocations across a nationwide chain can be a complex logistical puzzle.

Applebee's

Until mid-1999 Applebee's, a chain of more than 1,300 restaurants across the United States, plotted demand and distribution, marketing campaigns and the allocation of food product and staff by using spreadsheets and gut instinct. No particular consideration was given to regional or individual restaurant trends. Projections were generally linear. The result might be an equal distribution of porterhouse steaks among Applebee's restaurants in Maine and Texas. Then when the Texas restaurants ran out and the Maine restaurants were overstocked, the steaks were shipped for the second time, from Maine down to Texas.

Now Applebee's has centralized its information. Throughout the company there is access to historical performance by restaurant and product. Food stock, campaign management, staffing and costs can be tightly and accurately controlled. Unnecessary costs aren't cut. They are avoided. With this new internal information transparency, a higher return on investment is inevitable.

Without transparency between business units and adequate information, internal logistics can go wrong, erode trust and erode value. If, for example, a retailer's marketing department launches a major product campaign, stores need to be told. More companies than care to admit have been caught short by stealth marketing campaigns. Stock-outs are inevitable if the stores don't know a product is on special. Instead of creating a lift in sales, the marketing campaign results in dissatisfied customers who couldn't take advantage of the product offer. This erodes trust between company and consumer and internally between store buyers and the marketing group.

We've talked a lot about trust and information transparency as the basis for sound decision-making. Of course, the ultimate erosion of trust is fraud, but again information is the weapon to combat it. The better we understand our business, the tangibles of costs and the intangibles of "normal" behavior, the better we can prevent fraud. It's all part of the operational logistics of a company.

Fraud Prevention

Success is at jeopardy if fraud needlessly undercuts the value of a company. Information is absolutely essential to fraud prevention. How do we use it? Let's start with everyone's favorite government department—the tax man. Taxes and death, two sure things we can never escape. Except that tax evasion, tax fraud and innocent filing errors happen all the time.

In tough economic times with high unemployment rates and tight

Iowa Department of Revenue and Finance

government budgets, the Iowa Department of Revenue and Finance has invested time and money into centralizing and standardizing its information resources and using its improved understanding of the tax base to increase its revenues (that's "taxes" to the average person). Iowa's specific goals are:

- enhance voluntary compliance
- collect all taxes that are due
- manage the state's financial resources more efficiently

With better information, Iowa can analyze audit data and determine the cause of noncompliance.

- Was it an education issue?
- Was it a tax law issue?
- Was the tax form not clear?
- Or was it fraud?

Iowa Department of Revenue and Finance (cont'd.)   On the other side of the equation, Iowa can forecast the state's growth needs and analyze the impact of tax law changes before making the final decision to implement.

In a typical year the state processes more than 4 million documents. In 2001 it collected in excess of $5.8 billion from individuals and businesses and issued $538 million in refunds. In 2000 and 2001, the two years since it began its information initiative, Iowa has collected more than $20 million of new tax revenues from non-compliant taxpayers and the state anticipates increased revenues of $10 million annually.

Of course, information does not only help the government uncover fraud. Information also enables companies to track behavior patterns and see suspicious activity. A pattern of canceled "will-pay" subscriptions by the same subscriber. Early term claims on new insurance policies. Erratic credit card use.

Credit card fraud proliferates. Preventing it requires timely information and quick action. Most stolen credit cards hit their spending limit within 48 hours. So, detection needs to happen within minutes or it may already be too late. With timely information, on-the-spot analysis of current (potentially fraudulent) transactions combined with purchase history enables companies to react to behavior as it is happening.

For example, one pattern companies watch for is the use of a credit card for a purchase in which no people are involved. One traditional pattern is to test a stolen credit card on a gas pump, to make sure it works, and then begin using the card. Other patterns are sudden large purchases of consumer electronics, jewelry and airplane tickets. Credit card companies can flag these transactions, compare them with purchase history and react accordingly. Gauging the right reaction is important. A customer doesn't want their credit line cut off unnecessarily or to be contacted at every purchase. They also don't want a thief to spend their money. It's a delicate balance and striking it right has a direct impact on profitability.

Identifying and preventing fraud protects our hard-earned bottom line. We need to stay current. We can't rely on stale information. We are only ever one step ahead of the fraudsters, and their creativity will often match ours. The more information there is available, the better our decisions will be. Information and the power of our information resources enable us to control the difficult logistics and operational issues, and prevent fraud.

In the next chapter we'll change the angle of our perspective and look at a key issue that underlies every decision we make and is, ultimately, at the core of managing profitability—risk management.

CONTROL

6

Risk
Management

Ultimately, the decisions we make and the strategies we set must all be understood in terms of the risk we take. A decision is not only about cost and expected return. We have to factor in the risk that costs or returns are not as expected. We can only do this analysis effectively if we have a single view of our business.

Every company in every industry, financial or otherwise, deals with these three key areas of risk:

- Customer risk
- Market risk
- Operational risk

Risk Management 101

Customer risk is the internally generated risk that we lose customers or they act in a way that damages our business.

Market risk is the externally generated risk of surprises in the marketplace—downturns, recessions, inflation, volatility, normal business cycles, unexpected event triggers and other market conditions.

Operational risk refers to the category of internally generated risks that relate to systems failures and other operations-related surprises.

Customer risk, market risk and operational risk all derive from the same source—lack of information. Inadequate information means a company doesn't know enough about its customers to keep them. It means a company can't identify market trends. It means a company isn't in control of its internal operations. One factor underlies all the categories of risk—information. The less information a company has, the greater its risk.

> The number one risk factor
> in any organization is
> lack of accurate information.

Companies need strategies and systems in place to minimize the risk profile and maximize the wealth creation potential of all their relationships—customer, employee, partner and others. More than just the lifetime value of a relationship, the calculation of risk and return must include an "option value" of the potential relationship.

Option value, a relatively new valuation approach that is gaining currency in business, takes into account much more than the traditional straight-line-discounted, future value of an investment, or in this case a relationship. Option value also accounts for the potential returns of different possible paths, weighted according to their likelihood. It is a risk-return analysis that understands that multiple future possibilities exist for every investment and every relationship. A pharmaceutical company invests in research. The research may yield the expected results, or unexpected results. But unexpected results are not necessarily a sign of a lost investment. The results might lead the research in another direction that will pay off in the end, or it might not. Option analytics assigns a value to each of these potential paths. Relationship management at this level absolutely requires a company to have a single view of its business and a complete understanding of all its relationships.

Cultivating customers is the biggest reward potential most companies have. Accounting for the risk-return profile of customers is part of the new customer focus in the market. A single view of the business is essential to this calculation.

Here's one cautionary tale. A customer had multiple accounts with a bank—a small business account and a private banking account were just two of the relationship touch points. Whenever the customer had revenues in the small business account the customer moved it into the private banking account. The result was that the small business group didn't value the customer's business and the private banking group did.

Instead of seeing one relationship, the bank saw multiple relationships. The bank could not see the bigger picture of the customer's total value. The small business group advised the customer they were going to charge new, higher fees because the customer didn't maintain adequate account balances. The customer pointed out that there was an adequate balance in the private banking account at the same bank. The small business group, unimpressed, responded that as far as they were concerned the customer was not "valuable." The bank lost *all* of the customer's business.

Because the bank created a fragmented and ultimately unsatisfying relationship with its customer, it did not have a complete picture of its relationship to the customer. The bank was unable to assess the real *return* or the real *risks* associated with the customer.

Everything in a company should be focused on the bottom line—and that's the profitability of customers. Financial risk issues are not separate. They are part and parcel of the risk-return profile of a customer. Every company, financial or otherwise, needs to make its finance division a partner with the rest of the organization.

> An accurate customer profitability calculation must take into account the associated *risk* factors.

Risk management is about determining the right discount factor to account for the inherent risks taken to achieve a specific return. That means *knowing* your customers, the costs associated with maintaining the relationship and the risk of a change (either positive or negative) in that relationship. For example, a bank customer who uses a branch teller costs more to service than a customer who uses an ATM. But which of those two categories of customer tends to be more loyal? Unless that information is captured and available for analysis, any risk-return analysis will be fundamentally flawed.

A good risk management strategy is not just important to the bottom line. All companies, and financial institutions in particular, are rewarded disproportionately in the market for sound risk management practices. Stock prices go up. Shareholder value increases. On the flip side, the market exaggerates the risk profile of an unprepared company, which can send the stock value plunging.

Understanding the risk profile of customers is essential to any customer profitability driven business. In other words, it's important to every business. The financial industry has understood this longer than most. Unlike most other businesses, in financial services the customer can have a direct adverse impact on the business. In retail a customer may stop coming to a store, but in financial services a customer may default on their mortgage or a margin loan, leaving the company holding their debt.

Barclays Bank

At Barclays Bank the original impetus to centralize information resources was driven by their credit risk management needs. Being able to categorize the high, medium and low risk customers is critical to generating credit grades and risk-adjusted pricing, which is, after all, at the heart of their business. Credit risk *is* customer risk at a bank.

Financial services companies are required to abide by an array of credit risk regulations like the Basle II accord, a set of rules established in cooperation with the international financial community on credit risk issues. Economic capital analysis is intrinsic to the business. Barclays wants to know how much capital is allocated to each division of the business and the risk associated with that capital allocation. As with any financial services company, Barclays can't afford to risk *not knowing* enough about its customers.

Yet despite these risk management issues, banks have traditionally been horizontally siloed. Getting a snapshot of the true risk position of the institution on a customer-by-customer basis was virtually impossible. Credit card information was kept separate from mortgage information, which was separate from investment accounts and bank accounts. Insurance was completely cut off from the rest of the institution. In today's global market, financial institutions need to be more sensitive to their customers' complete risk profiles.

The traditionally siloed nature of the financial industry was due, in part, to the regulatory climate. Regulations are changing and so is the financial industry in general.

TowerGroup

Mark Sievewright, President and CEO of the TowerGroup, says that one of the key areas of focus of any financial institution today has to be wealth management. The baby boom generation is the single most important target market. The demographic significance of the baby boomers for every industry cannot be underestimated. As Harry Dent has so colorfully put it, tracking the boomer demographic over time is like watching a pig move through a python.

Wealth management brings together banking, investment and insurance—the full range of the financial industry's offerings.

Sievewright describes the new reality of the financial industry with his "Five C's":

- Consolidation
- Convergence
- Customer Focus
- Channels
- Cost of Ownership

In 1980 the top 20 banks held 19.5 percent of total assets. In 1998 that figure had doubled to 39.8 percent. The top 50 banks currently control more than 71.2 percent of total assets, more than twice what they controlled twenty years ago. The drive to consolidate comes from three key sources: the motivation to maximize value through economies of scale and scope, cost efficiencies and "monopoly" power. The result is that banks need an overwhelming amount of information to be able to understand their customers.

The natural outgrowth of successful consolidation is convergence. Citibank is number one globally, across the range of potential strategic focus for a financial institution—global credit cards, global consumer finance, emerging markets, global capital markets and global wealth management. Yet convergence creates its own challenges: the question of integration vs. co-existence, channel conflicts, branding conflicts and culture clashes. As with consolidation, convergence will only be successful with an information structure that centralizes and disseminates all the data in the company.

Sievewright believes, with the next wave of businesses, expanding scale and scope will be achieved through partnerships and alliances, not mergers and acquisitions. Lower risk and more agile partners are a way of dealing with the need to consolidate and converge without the drawbacks of massive size. Partnerships and alliances may also be a superior method of dealing with the third "C" in the new market reality, customer focus.

TowerGroup (cont'd.)

Becoming customer-centric is one of the surest ways to increase return on investment. A customer focus needs to be embedded into the business processes. The emphasis on customers at most companies was lost in the rush to adopt all sorts of new technologies and to get online. What companies forgot was that technology is not an end in itself. Technology serves a function and that function, at its core, should be to serve the customer better.

True customer focus leads naturally to the fourth "C," channels. To be truly customer-centric, a customer's experience dealing with a company across all channels should be seamless.

Finally, in the fast-paced global economy of today, return on investment must happen quickly and be visible. Cost accountability is higher than ever. Companies need to decide which cost model works best for them and mine its opportunities—outsourcing vs. in-house. CTOs have fewer chances to get "IT" right.

Sievewright's "Five C's" provide important insight into understanding any financial institution's overall risk management strategy, and financial institutions are the best examples of risk management in practice. But every company needs to realize that, in the end, everything comes down to risk management. Have a strategy.

> Every interaction, connection and transaction is a potential risk.

Every industry, financial or otherwise, has risk factors built into the very nature of its business.

- Were deliveries on time?
- Was mobile phone service interrupted?
- Did a customer leave unsatisfied?
- Did a stolen credit card get used?

These are all risks and it is only by using our information that we can stay on top of them.

A single view of the business is *the* prerequisite to a smooth-functioning corporate ecosystem. We've seen it with customers, logistics and operations in previous chapters. Now we've seen the important role of information resources in risk management. What does all this mean to the bottom line? We'll look at this in the next chapter.

VALUE

7

Insight, Oversight and Higher Returns

How much do you really know about the financial condition of your company?

Most of us monitor the financial health of our companies quarterly. We finalize budgets for the next year two months before the year even starts, which means we're predicting performance 14 months in advance. Then we do three-year plans and five-year plans. No matter how good our information is, can we really say that we know what's going to happen three years from now? Is it good business to pretend we can see into the future? Not necessarily. Not only is the value of long-range financial planning overrated, it can often lead to slack oversight. "It's in the plan" is not a good enough reason to do something that no longer makes bottom-line sense.

Establishing a strategic plan, the bedrock vision of where the company should be, is always valuable. Attaching hard numbers to that corporate vision can actually limit our ability to respond to change quickly. Being agile is essential in the market today. We need to know more, and know faster, about the financials of our companies. We need to bind ourselves to long-range forecasts less.

Of course we're not advocating that quarterly and annual statements be abandoned. Not only are they legally required, they are critical to getting the big picture. But the most important financial information may not be in the "financials." We need to drill down into the numbers and we need to do it regularly.

> We need to know about revenue,
> order and expense run rate
> right now to be able to recommend
> timely action before we close
> the books, when it will have
> the most impact.

Continental President Larry Kellner **Continental Airlines**
has an array of financial information
at his fingertips on his desktop computer every day. He can track
performance on an almost hourly basis. He can dig into the
regional numbers, the country numbers and individual flights to
pinpoint successes and problem areas. That means Kellner can
take action immediately when he spots an issue. He doesn't have
to wait until quarterly numbers come and then spend time asking
for details. By then it's too late to take effective action. The
window of opportunity has passed.

Recession Opportunity

Opportunities come in two styles. There are growth opportunities and
there are recession opportunities. The latter are frequently overlooked or
mischaracterized as cost-cutting measures only. Managing well in a down
economy takes more than squeezing costs. Top leaders are always looking
for opportunity and that requires detailed information available early
enough to make a difference.

At any company the question in a down economy is how to
approach customers whose profits are declining and get a bigger share of
their business.

FedEx has grown its revenue base **FedEx**
despite lean economic times.
Considering the long lead times FedEx needs to establish
distribution facilities, and buy planes and trucks, their stability in
hard times is doubly impressive.

FedEx CIO Rob Carter's advice—don't fly blind. It is more critical
than ever in a changing economy to see where the company is
going. If there's less package traffic through Kuala Lumpur, then

FedEx (cont'd.)

smaller planes need to be assigned to that location. If there's less package traffic from and to Kansas, then reshape the network to move more packages *through* Kansas, making use of the state's facilities.

How does FedEx know what the right decisions are? FedEx has continued to invest in its decision support environment to ensure that its information superhub provides the most value possible.

At FedEx, information is the secret to continued success through ups and downs in the market.

Financial Reporting

Of course, when we have detail data available daily, preparing the quarterly and annual numbers and budgeting becomes a much more efficient process. Not only can we have more accurate reports earlier, we can save money.

We've seen it repeated across many industries in these pages: Detail data is essential. The better insight we have into our businesses, the better oversight. That's critical in today's environment. Shareholders' faith in corporations has been eroded. At worst they believe we lie, and at best they think we don't really understand our business. The truth is, if we don't have detailed, accurate, timely information, we probably don't understand our businesses as well as we should. We need to regain the public's trust. Fortunately rebuilding public trust is also good for the bottom line.

Better insight ➡ Better oversight ➡ Higher value

Getting Results

Gaining better insight will produce great financial results. We've seen throughout the extraordinary performance records by companies who committed their business to information, who are leveraging their information resources to better understand their customers, suppliers, partners and the market.

> *We are witnessing a migration in value from the resources that were once the basis of competitive advantage…physical assets and physical resources, toward the new sources for competitive advantage, intangible assets…human capital, structural capital and relationship capital.*

Experts Say

Mohanbir Sawhney
McCormick Tribune Professor
of Technology
Kellogg School of Management
at Northwestern University

The value potential of intangible assets is unlocked by information. Employee empowerment breeds high performance and loyalty. Logistical efficiency maximizes supplier relationships. Open communication creates effective alliances and partnerships.

The companies who have made the commitment to information are financially fittest because they are best able to adapt to new market imperatives. The business world after all is no different than anything else—the fittest survive.

As if the case studies we've looked at already haven't been extraordinary enough, here are just a few more companies whose bottom-line value soared when they began capitalizing on their information.

In Canada, Royal Bank of Canada (RBC) has raised the art and science of customer relationships to new levels of achievement. The improvements in economic profit are proof of their leadership.

RBC

Between 1999 and 2001 RBC achieved enviable results:

- 32 percent improvement in economic profit in its key market segment (the early life stage customers)
- 61 percent improvement in its prime market segment (the wealth accumulators and preservers)
- 138 percent improvement in its growth market segment (mid-cycle customers, builders and borrowers)

At Travelocity, the online travel company's aggressive use of its information resources to improve its relationship with customers has proved valuable.

Travelocity

In 2000, Travelocity's:

- Conversion for recipients of targeted event-driven campaigns improved by up to 400 percent
- Conversion for newsletter subscribers improved by 84 percent
- Booker conversion rates rose to 8.9 percent

Finally, in Brazil, BCP Telecommunications, a Brazilian Bellsouth affiliated company with almost three million customers, has scored some big wins.

BCP Telecommunications

Using its information resources in new customer acquisition initiatives, BCP Telecommunications has returned, in these tougher times in the telecom industry, stellar results:

- Plan penetration has increased 8.5 percent
- Insurance penetration has increased 12.6 percent

- Revenues are 100 percent higher
- Churn is 64 percent lower
- The cost per account is 22.1 percent lower
- The number of months in which an acquisition campaign pays back is 10 percent lower

In fact, for every dollar spent now on marketing, the company earns revenues of $4 within 12 months.

Leveraging its information sources has paid off handsomely for BCP.

Better insight, better oversight and higher returns—we can't afford not to invest in our information resources.

VISION

8

The Next
Frontiers

Are we there yet?

We know what we need to do. We understand the power of our information resources and the enormous value potential. But knowing this and *implementing* a strategy for using our information resources are two different things. We still have a long way to go. Throughout this book we've looked at top companies that are acting on the vision, but none of us are using our information to its full potential. There's work to be done. We haven't fully committed to our information resources yet. Many large companies are still struggling to sort through the flood of data and get a single view of the business. It's a process that takes time, commitment and energy, from the CEO to the front lines.

The statistics are revealing:

- 54 percent of U.S. business executives say their data is doubling and tripling every year.
- 73 percent say it's not easy to navigate, understand or use the data they know they have.
- 73 percent say they made more daily decisions this year than they did last year.

That's the executive level. At the employee level, the statistics are reinforced:

- 75 percent of workers say they miss opportunities because they don't make decisions fast enough.
- Only 25 percent of workers believe that their organization is moving faster than its competitors.

The trend is against us if we don't stay on top of our information. Leveraging our information is not about technology. It's about how we want to manage our companies. The company with the best understanding of its customers, its processes and its organization is going to win.

We understand intuitively how to run our businesses in near real-time. Now we need to execute on that understanding. We need to envision beyond that goal. Our new motto should be "foresight is 20/20." Even a recent series of print ads for Nasdaq shows quotes on this popular theme. In one ad Bruce Chizen, President and CEO of Adobe Systems Inc., is quoted, "If you want to make history, create the future." In another, Bruce Carter, President and CEO of ZymoGenetics, is quoted as saying, "True vision is the ability to see things that don't yet exist." What we need to do is on the tip of everyone's tongues, but it has yet to be truly executed.

Retail, manufacturing, shipping, airlines, financial services and every other industry will be called upon to use its information resources more effectively and efficiently or fall behind. The speed and volume of information accumulation must be met with ever-greater ingenuity.

> *The demands on capacity and speed are increasing exponentially as free trade continues to expand on a global basis.*

Experts Say

Klaus Zumwinkel
Deutsche Post World Net
Chairman of the Board
of Management

Information resources will drive the next phase of improved productivity in business. Companies will move from using information strategically to using information tactically. Strategic decisions have always relied on the information a company has about its past performance. The assumptions a company made about the future were based on analyses of historical data. But the most successful strategies require that information be used for the day-to-day tactical decisions. Real-time flexible reactive and proactive decision-making means using information tactically to successfully execute strategy.

Business fundamentals haven't changed. In fact, as the market accelerates and speed of decision-making becomes ever more critical, it is increasingly important to refocus on the core business drivers of our companies. We need to be faster and leaner, but we don't need to change our business basics.

Retailers need to continue getting closer to their suppliers and partners, opening up the supply chain process, shaving inventory and restocking more responsively. Manufacturing needs to continue closing the gap between factory and consumer. The logistics sector needs to keep meeting the challenges of steadily higher growth in global distribution networks as national boundaries become ever more permeable. Financial services needs to continue working to be more relevant to customers. We all need to be more transparent in our business operations. The more freely information flows, the more fulsome our information resources, the more questions we can answer. Answers mean opportunities.

We need to ask questions we don't know the answers to today and then ask even harder questions.

Financial

- How can I improve share price in any economy?
- Where are new product introductions not getting results?
- How do I know that when I sign off on financial documents they're accurate?
- How can I drill the financial detail to redirect, streamline and cut costs?
- How can I improve margins, pricing, inventory and accounts receivable to get better cash flow?
- How can I better sweat my assets and leverage return on capital?

Operations

- Is there a way to reduce our cycle times?
- Can we reduce back-order situations by leveraging all our inventory and capacity?
- Which of my distributors is contributing to profitable growth?
- Can we leverage our total procurement power to cut spending?

Sales and Marketing

- Where are my profitable relationships?
- Where are my sales performance deficiencies?
- Where can we increase market penetration?
- What are the opportunities to improve customer penetration and reduce churn?
- Where are new customer and market prospects?
- Are retention programs working as well as they should?

All of us can answer some of these questions right now. None of us can answer them all right now. The company that gets there first will have an enormous competitive advantage. This is the information we need to begin using tactically and not just strategically. Information transparency is a long-term strategy and a tactical necessity. In these pages we've seen that many top companies are already on course for dramatic improvements in productivity. Still more can be achieved.

Corporate Structure

Though business fundamentals aren't changing, the ways we think about and structure our businesses do need to change if we are to compete and grow.

Mohanbir Sawhney   One leading expert who has done
a lot of thinking about the changes
we can make is Mohanbir Sawhney, McCormick Tribune Professor
of Technology at Northwestern University's Kellogg School of
Management. His insights into how we need to approach our
businesses are invaluable. Sawhney says we need to recognize
that what he calls "relational equity" is the new wealth of the
corporation. The intangible value of the relationships a
company builds is in many cases more important than the
tangible "things" that are measured on the balance sheet. The
result—companies are structured around the things on their
balance sheets, around assets and objects, instead of around the
relationships, which are the most valuable assets of the company.

Companies, Sawhney says, need to become as efficient at
managing relationships as they are about managing things.
Corporate structure needs to reflect this new mandate. He points
out three old ideas that drive current structural norms and that
stand in the way of success.

1. Product superiority drives success. This, he says, is an
    outdated notion and should not dictate corporate focus and
    structure.
2. Product differentiation distinguishes between competitors.
    Wrong, says Sawhney. Products have become too complicated
    for customers and for the most part competitors have
    reached feature parity.
3. Complexity in the product portfolio provides choice and
    range that attract customers. Not so. The number of
    customer segments has not increased commensurately with
    the number of different products. Instead, customers are
    inundated by products with indistinguishable variations.

We need, Sawhney says, to understand and measure the value of relationships. For example, he suggests five new approaches to quantifying customer value.

1. *Total value* over the relationship's lifetime.
2. *Potential value*, including potential revenues from products and services a company could offer in the future as well as existing product lines.
3. *Profitability* of the relationship.
4. *Insights* a customer can provide have value. The knowledgeable feedback on new products and marketplace trends that, for example, early adopters can often offer is a valuable resource.
5. *Influence* a customer wields over other customers has value. Opinion leaders and influencers are most valuable for the business they can bring in, not for the business they do with you.

All relationships—with partners, customers and employees— appreciate, depreciate, are subject to risk and have option value. We need to replace the balanced scorecard with a relational scorecard. Replace the product lifecycle with a relational lifecycle. Structure our portfolio of relationships, not products.

Restructuring to reflect this change of focus does not mean destroying the functional or product silos around which most companies are structured. It involves making the silos *permeable* to information sharing. Information is the lubricant in all our relationships. We need to structure and manage our companies to capture and use the extensive information we can harvest from our relationships. But Sawhney's analysis does not stop there.

Mohanbir Sawhney (cont'd.)   Capturing and using relationship information quickly, doing business in so-called "real-time," is the Next Big Thing touted by the business media. The analysts call it the Real-Time Enterprise. Sawhney cautions against jumping on the bandwagon and prescribes the following reality checks:

1. The idea is not new.
2. The capability is not real, yet. Change will necessarily be slow and incremental.
3. To achieve real-time is not about the single company. It requires seamless connections between suppliers, partners and customers.
4. Real-time is not about speed. It's about speed for a purpose—creating additional value.
5. Technology is not the solution. It is a tool.
6. To achieve real-time is not the right goal for every company.

The bottom line is to maximize the potential of our information resources by developing effective methods of capturing important data and then to find the most valuable way to use the information resources gleaned from our relationships. There is no one-size-fits-all solution, but to succeed every company needs to work toward the new relational paradigm.

Security and Privacy

Information resources can also be the key to the many pressing security and privacy issues we face.

In the airline industry, for example, the hot issue is security. Pilots, crew and passengers all want to feel safe in the air. They also want to be able to fly with a minimum of fuss and time expenditure. There is a fine balance between security and service. Some statistics suggest that the passengers who are most searched are often the highest paying, a figure that does not bode well for service satisfaction ratings. Vast sums of money are being invested in the security infrastructure of airlines.

Effective, efficient security requires profiling and differentiating both employees and customers. Making material distinctions between people will only be possible with a great deal of information from a variety of sources—internal, other airlines, other companies, other countries and government agencies. Many companies are starting to hire Chief Security Officers (CSOs) to work on solutions to the problem. Without good information, no solutions are possible.

Governments have work to do on many fronts, security in particular. International information collaboration between governments and within governments can enable international and domestic agencies to effectively track criminals, including terrorists. The bigger the information trail, the more likely it is that criminals will be detected *before* they commit a crime.

Of course, privacy issues must be addressed simultaneously. Fortunately, protecting the security of personal information is well within the capability of currently available tools and infrastructure. The only obstacle is commitment.

The Health Insurance Portability and Accountability Act, a new federal law that creates security standards to ensure the privacy of patients' medical records, has already forced doctors, hospitals, health-care providers, insurance companies and biotechnology companies to shore up their privacy protection. The real creativity and excitement will come in how, once privacy is secured, the vast stores of medical information can be used to advance our understanding of disease and find cures.

Salk Institute

On the medical frontiers at the Salk Institute, Dr. Carolee Barlow's research into brain diseases requires her to analyze an extraordinary amount of data. As scientific instruments have improved, the volume of data has multiplied inordinately. It is now possible for Dr. Barlow to measure exactly how much RNA is generated by each gene in each of the literally trillions of cells in the brain and to derive individual gene expression profiles.

Dr. Barlow's particular field of interest is neurological disorders in human beings. Much of her research has focused on identifying the differences in the gene expression profile of a strain of mouse known to be anxious and a strain of mouse known to be bold and curious. In doing this she hopes to identify the genes associated with crippling anxiety in humans.

To compound the information issue, what interests Dr. Barlow in all this data is not what might interest another neuroscientist working on a different disease. The process of separating "signal" from "noise" in all this data yields entirely different results depending on the research focus.

Dr. Barlow compares the nature of her search for answers to the issues a Wal-Mart faces doing market-basket analysis. With the same tools at her disposal that Wal-Mart uses, namely the ability to ask hundreds of unexpected questions of the data, Dr. Barlow is able to work with previously difficult to manage data sets. And the flexibility that enables Dr. Barlow to work with the data allows any doctor to ask questions, even on totally different issues. Both doctors can look at the same information for different purposes and derive extraordinary value.

Progress in the ability to store enormous volumes of information and access it in flexible formats might just be one of the tickets to breaking through new medical frontiers.

We're not there yet. But we're heading in the right direction. The project of capitalizing on our information resources is organic. As we move toward our ultimate goal of real-time, perhaps even anticipatory, decision-making, the goalposts move too. There will always be ways in which we can run our companies better, be more competitive and achieve higher growth and profits. Fortunately for us that means our jobs as CEOs and senior executives will be challenging and interesting for a long time to come.

Creativity, ingenuity, vision and common business sense are ever in demand.

INDEX

ABOUT THE AUTHORS

Mark Hurd is president and chief executive officer of NCR Corporation, a leading global technology company. NCR's automated teller machines, retail systems, Teradata® data warehouses and IT services provide Relationship Technology™ solutions that maximize the value of customer interactions.

Hurd was named chief executive officer and elected to the board in March 2003. Previously, as president and chief operating officer he was instrumental in formulating and executing strategies to maximize operating efficiencies and profitability.

Hurd joined NCR in 1980 and was chosen to run the Teradata division in October 1999. He was promoted to chief operating officer of the division within a year. Under Hurd's leadership, Teradata increased revenue by approximately 36 percent and improved operating performance by over $250 million. Today, Teradata is a $1.2 billion business and the market leader in large data warehouses and analytical solutions that help businesses drive growth.

Lars Nyberg is chairman of the board of directors of NCR Corporation, a leading provider of Relationship Technology™ solutions.

Nyberg served as NCR's chief executive officer from June 1995 until March 2003, and led its transformation from a hardware manufacturer to a technology solutions provider. He also is widely acknowledged as the architect of NCR's dramatic turnaround following its spin-off from AT&T at the end of 1996. Today, the company is a global technology leader and number one worldwide in data warehouses above one terabyte in size, automated teller machines and stationary barcode scanners.

Prior to joining NCR, Nyberg spent 20 years with Philips Electronics NV in a number of senior positions. Most recently, he was chairman and CEO of Philips' Communications Systems Division. Nyberg also serves on the boards of directors of The Sandvik Group in Sweden and Wisconsin-based Snap-on Incorporated.

ABOUT BLOOMBERG

Bloomberg L.P., founded in 1981, is a global information services, news, and media company. Headquartered in New York, the company has nine sales offices, two data centers, and 94 news bureaus worldwide.

Bloomberg, serving customers in 126 countries around the world, holds a unique position within the financial services industry by providing an unparalleled range of features in a single package known as the BLOOMBERG PROFESSIONAL® service. By addressing the demand for investment performance and efficiency through an exceptional combination of information, analytic, electronic trading, and Straight Through Processing tools, Bloomberg has built a worldwide customer base of corporations, issuers, financial intermediaries, and institutional investors.

BLOOMBERG NEWS®, founded in 1990, provides stories and columns on business, general news, politics, and sports to leading newspapers and magazines throughout the world. BLOOMBERG TELEVISION®, a 24-hour business and financial news network, is produced and distributed globally in seven different languages. BLOOMBERG RADIO℠ is an international radio network anchored by flagship station BLOOMBERG® 1130 (WBBR-AM) in New York.

In addition to the BLOOMBERG PRESS® line of books, Bloomberg publishes *BLOOMBERG MARKETS®* and *BLOOMBERG WEALTH MANAGER®*. To learn more about Bloomberg, call a sales representative at:

Frankfurt:	49-69-92041-0	São Paulo:	5511-3048-4500
Hong Kong:	852-2977-6000	Singapore:	65-6212-1000
London:	44-20-7330-7500	Sydney:	61-2-9777-8600
New York:	1-212-318-2000	Tokyo:	81-3-3201-8900
San Francisco:	1-415-912-2960		

FOR IN-DEPTH MARKET INFORMATION and news, visit the Bloomberg website at **www.bloomberg.com**, which draws from the news and power of the BLOOMBERG PROFESSIONAL® service and Bloomberg's host of media products to provide high-quality news and information in multiple languages on stocks, bonds, currencies, and commodities.